Meal Stories

The Gospel
of Our Lives

Meal Stories

The Gospel of Our Lives

Kathleen Casey

ThomasMore®
Allen, Texas

Acknowledgments:

Cover Design: Pamela Glick Creative Design & Illustration

Text Design: Laura Fremder

Cover Photo: © PhotoDisc

The Scripture quotations contained herein are from the *New Revised Standard Version Bible: Catholic Edition* copyright © 1993 and 1989 by the Division of Christian Education for the National Council of the Churches of Christ in the U.S.A. Used by permission. All rights reserved.

Send all inquiries to:
Thomas More® Publishing
An RCL Company
200 East Bethany Drive
Allen, Texas 75002-3804

Telephone: 800-264-0368 / 972-390-6300
Fax: 800-688-8356 / 972-390-6560

Visit us at: **www.thomasmore.com**
Customer Service E-mail: **cservice@rcl-enterprises.com**

Printed in the United States of America

Library of Congress Control Number: 2002109703

7495   ISBN 0-88347-495-6

1 2 3 4 5   06 05 04 03 02

*To my family, friends,
and patients, who have all
been my teachers.*

"According to the gospels, Jesus never ate alone. According to Kathleen Casey, a specialist in pediatric feeding and swallowing: 'Eating alone may feed the body but not the soul.' She maintains that when you accept food from another and share it with others you develop intimacy. The meals Jesus ate with others in the gospels fed their souls. This book will feed the souls of all who read it."

—Arthur E. Zannoni

"Reading *Meal Stories* is like making a wonderful, inspiring retreat! Casey has connected the dots of life in this book, returning us to a sense that all the dimensions of our lives are truly integrated and tied together. She inserts the spiritual into everyday living. This book might just change your life!"

—Bill Huebsch

Contents

Foreword

ONCE YOU LOOK AT IT, it is surprising—to some even shocking—how "unreligious" Jesus is. He does not fit our later definitions of a pious or churchy person at all. In fact, almost half of the gospel stories illustrate direct conflict with the establishment of his own religion. He is not an "ordained" rabbi; he is not from the priestly class; and he usually does his teaching in nonreligious settings and in "street" language.

Jesus is a layman who trusts his own experience of God both within his Jewish tradition and yet often against that very tradition. He is both a loyalist and an utter critic of his own religion. Normally, this is the word for a prophet. A prophet has a different perspective than that of the priest or even the pious layperson. It is the preferred perspective of Jesus, and maybe what finally gets him killed. It also makes him universal and utterly accessible, if you are interested in such things—I have found that many church people are not.

The prophet is not as concerned about the temple or the synagogue as he is the city, the street, and the home. His podium is not inside a formal liturgical space, but at the places of social interaction, the town square, the battlefield, the royal court, the tax collector's table, and in the basic social unit—at the family meal. Not surprisingly, the major Jewish feasts are celebrated, at least in part, around that same family table. The sacred and the secular must be made one and the same—or religion is largely impotent. "Hear, O Israel: The LORD is our God, the LORD alone," says Deuteronomy 6:4. And the job of the prophet is the same as that of the mystic—to make all things one. They both offer one utterly integrated worldview to a world that prefers to split, separate, compartmentalize, and divide. Prophets and mystics are the true and original and ultimate ecologists.

As you study the four gospels, it is obvious that Jesus often uses the small meal setting to present many of his major teachings, his major criticisms, and his major rituals. The meal seems to be his audio-visual aid whereby he redefines and realigns the social order. It has been said that he is always eating the wrong thing, with the wrong people, in the wrong place, in the wrong table setting, and after not washing his hands! He uses meal settings in several of his most poignant parables, and often uses food or kitchen language as a primary metaphor (salt, yeast, dough, wine, water, wineskins, kneading, drinking, etc.). The will of God itself is described as his "food," and the word of God more nourishing than bread. This is not clerical language; in fact, it is not even typical male language. Jesus is a most unusual founder for a religion that became very religious, very liturgical, very clerical, and very patriarchal. In fact, one wonders sometimes how the two are even connected.

Well, Kathleen Casey is going to help you make this connection anew. Like every good mystic, every good prophet, and every true teacher of Jesus, she is going to put back together what has been separated and disconnected. She is going to help us make it all ONE again, so, as it was among most ancient peoples, there is no real word for "religion." It is just life, and life in abundance, and life everywhere, and in every moment. Like God.

And the final words of the prophet Zechariah will be fulfilled: "On that day there shall be inscribed on the bells of the horses, 'Holy to the LORD.' And the cooking pots in the house of the LORD shall be as holy as the bowls in front of the altar; and every cooking pot in Jerusalem and Judah shall be sacred to the LORD of hosts . . ." (Zechariah 14:20–21).

This is where we are heading! And this book is heading in the same direction. Read and eat and be satisfied.

—Richard Rohr, O.F.M.
Center for Action and Contemplation
Albuquerque, New Mexico

1

Vocation

When we find our true vocation,
work no longer interferes with prayer or prayer with work.
Contemplation no longer needs a special state
that removes us from the ordinary things around us,
for God penetrates all.
THOMAS MERTON

WE ALL WEAR SO MANY HATS these days and we identify ourselves by these hats. I remember one day in particular. I came home from work, helped the kids with their homework, made dinner, and then tried to help a patient who called with a problem. After that I spent a few minutes making phone calls for a church event. I was finished just in time to get the kids upstairs for their bedtime routine. My husband said to me that night that he thought it was amazing how easily I slipped out of one role and into another.

My name is Kathleen Casey.

I am the wife of Thom.

I am the mother of Michele and Brian.

I am the daughter of Bob and Jeanne.

I am the sister of Bob, Jack, Tom, Bruce, Jeanne, Betty, Emily, Frank, and Christine.

I am a parishioner of St. Gabriel Church.
I am a speech language pathologist.
But mostly, I am a child of God.

What would it be like if being a child of God was the only way I was identified? How would life be different? Of course all these titles or roles can help us relate to each other, to find common bonds. But they can also keep us apart. The great equalizer is that we are all children; we are all creations of God. I need these roles to tell you who I am and how I came to write this little book. In the end, what I have found for myself is that these roles are all just facets of me and that the only full description of me is that I am a child of God.

I was raised Catholic, the eighth of ten children. I was a born cynic. Growing up I asked a million questions about the beliefs and practices of the church. I was frustrated with the typical answers of "it's just what we believe," or "because that's what the church teaches." We went to church every Sunday and on holy days, and we went to confession frequently. When I was a teenager our parish priest asked for volunteers for eucharistic ministry. I worked up the nerve to volunteer but was told that the altar was no place for women. I got the distinct impression that this priest would have liked to exclude women from the church entirely. That was enough for me.

Although I continued to go to Mass with my parents, it was at that time that I really left the church. I searched for a church that welcomed me and challenged me. I went East. I dabbled in Buddhism and found many similarities to Catholicism. By nature I was drawn to self-reflection and discipline. One of the things that was most attractive to me was that Buddhists didn't give pat answers. Life was a mystery. It was okay not to know. The world was innerconnected; the patterns repeated; each one of us was part of a bigger whole, and this was enough. There was also an emphasis on silence and solitude, which I craved. It was a place where I could stop questioning, analyzing, and problem solving. I could finally relax—it gave me a sense of peace. There were no Sanghas (churches or groups of people practicing the principles together) in my area so there was no sense of community for me. It felt as if we were reaching for enlightenment independently.

It was also difficult for me to give up on the conviction that Jesus is our Savior. By faith or enculturation or both, I was Christian. I tried then to find a home in the Presbyterian, Baptist, and Methodist churches. I remember distinctly going to a service and thinking how wonderful it was to celebrate Jesus. They were incredibly hospitable and welcoming. It made me wonder if they got extra points for converting a Catholic! I would invariably leave the service feeling I had a better understanding of the scripture. It was refreshing to give up the notion that we can work our way into heaven. Although Catholicism doesn't teach this, our practices suggest that this is just what we are trying to do.

After the service I wanted to say, "You forgot something." I wasn't quite sure what it was, but it was important. In the meantime, the priest where I went to college tried to get me to come back to Mass. We talked a few times and I told him about my experiences in the church. He handed me a book on the proceedings and the documents of Vatican II and said, "Read these." When I returned the books I said, "That's a great church; it's just not the Catholic Church." He challenged me to come to Mass one time. His was a post-Vatican II church with a little southern gospel thrown in.

When they started the Liturgy of the Eucharist I realized what I was missing. In the other churches, we had prayed side by side and rejoiced together; but we had not served each other; we had not shared a meal. For me we had not become a community. I thought how great it would be to combine the welcoming and celebration and true witness of the Protestant churches with the formation of community that is brought about through sharing the Eucharist. I found that the combination of celebration, challenge and community did exist. This Mass was a joyous event and the community was primary.

Amazingly, like Dorothy in the Wizard of Oz, I had found my home and it was right where I had left it. I was also welcomed as a leader of the church even though I was female. I became involved in a half-dozen social ministries. I arranged outings for adults in a home for the disabled, Bible studies with prison inmates, and I volunteered as an interpreter at the nearby school for the deaf. Finally, what brought it full circle for me was being asked to serve my community as a eucharistic minister. Each time I assisted with communion, I felt honored to give such a precious gift to each and every student.

What I didn't learn until years later was that as I visited the adult home, the prison, and the school, I was giving and receiving eucharist there, too, all along. The Eucharist has always been, whether I was aware of it or not, an integral part of my faith. It renews me and reminds me of God's love for each of us; it challenges me to live out that love; and it keeps me hopeful for the day we will all be present at the banquet.

IN COLLEGE and graduate school I trained to be a speech language pathologist. I chose speech pathology because I felt that not being able to communicate would be the worst kind of prison and I wanted to help relieve people of that burden. When I left graduate school for my first job, I had visions of conquering the world. I went to work at the Richmond Cerebral Palsy Center with my dreams and ambition. What I got was a big dose of reality.

I learned very quickly that I couldn't "cure" these children. I couldn't take away the nearly insurmountable challenges that they and their families live with everyday. I could just barely make it a little better. However, I also found that I could make them smile and on a good day I could help them tell their mom or dad that they loved them.

Shortly after starting work there, I became disturbed by the children's frequent bouts of aspiration pneumonia. This kind of pneumonia is caused by food or liquid going down the wrong way and infecting the lungs. They often battle chronic respiratory infections and it is a common cause of death. It was considered just a part of having cerebral palsy (CP). It prompted me to start working with children who had dysphagia—swallowing problems. For more than a dozen years now I've been working in a hospital with infants and adults who have dysphagia.

I work with infants who are born prematurely and have anatomical defects or syndromes and with children who are chronically ill or have handicapping conditions. I also work with adults who have suffered a stroke or undergone head, neck, or heart surgery; as well as those with Parkinson's, Lou Gehrig's Disease (ALS), and a myriad of other disorders which carry dysphagia as a complication. I'm called a feeding specialist. In my job I am often involved with families as they face traumatic events, dramatic changes in lifestyle, and end-of-life decisions.

What I have come to learn is that communication means far more than the movements of bones, tissues, and muscles; and eating is so much more than swallowing.

Even though I had been a feeding specialist and a eucharistic minister for many years, I did not relate the two until one day six or seven years ago when I was at work. I received a consult for a patient who was in the cardiac surgical intensive care unit (CSICU). I am asked to see patients after surgeries to evaluate their readiness to resume oral feeding. The patient had just had the breathing tube removed from his airway after a complicated surgery. He still had a risky recovery ahead of him.

All morning the patient and his family had been anxiously awaiting my arrival. They had brought in all his favorite foods with the hope that he would be able to eat something. I had only been there long enough to introduce myself to the patient and his family when he went into respiratory arrest. By the time I reached the button to call the code blue, the code team was racing in. As you might imagine, this is very traumatic for the family as people are rushing around, not meaning to push them aside, to attend to the patient.

I ushered them out of the room as quickly as I could while preparing myself to be bombarded with the inevitable questions about life and death. Instead, I was totally unprepared for the very first and only question they asked, "Will this stop you from letting him eat with us?" After so many years of feeding at work, at home, and in church, in that instant, I put it all together and realized what sharing a meal really meant. To this family it was their assurance that their father, husband, friend would be okay, and that once again they would be a family. It was symbolic of life itself.

After this experience, as I distribute communion, I am so grateful to a God who chose to use such earthy symbols to communicate his desire to be family with us, to have life with us. I wonder when I hand the body or blood of Christ to individuals in my community if they appreciate the profound wisdom and simplicity of these symbols. To eat together is to be intimate and vulnerable to each other. Sharing a meal is the deepest and most universal sign of unity and it was given to us by a truly loving God.

RECENTLY, I started to look at the meal stories in the gospels and I found that Jesus taught many of his lessons in the midst of a meal. In the gospel of Luke alone there are ten meal stories and many more references to eating and drinking.

There are two kinds of meal stories, one with bread and wine, the other with bread and fish. At the meals with bread and wine Jesus eats with the rich and the poor, with sinners and church officials alike. His message seems to be one of inclusion, an opening of the doors, but also confrontation with one's true self; and then compassion and forgiveness.

The fish and loaves stories speak of social justice. In each version, when the disciples suggest it is time for the people to leave to fend for themselves, Jesus counters with a challenge to his disciples. He says, "Feed them yourselves." These meals also send a message about surplus. There are always seven or twelve baskets left over. These numbers are used symbolically, I'm sure, as they are elsewhere in scripture. The number seven signifies holiness or divinity, so these meals are a foreshadowing of the kingdom banquet. The number twelve suggests wholeness, completeness, like the twelve tribes of Israel. The message for me is one of a universal church.

Both kinds of meal stories depict the deepest messages of the gospel for me and I find the gospel message being lived out in the lives of my patients every day. In an effort to make myself more aware of the moments of grace that fill my life, I have made it part of my prayer discipline to reflect on the ordinary events of my day in the light of scripture. These short stories are a product of this effort (I will use fictitious names for privacy reasons). I include excerpts from my daily prayer journal as well as insights I have gathered from many scripture scholars.

Jesus, help me balance the active and the quiet aspects of my life,
recognizing both as a way of prayer.
Give me grace to seek times of quiet contemplation
to sustain me when my prayer
is the work you give me to do in the world.
MARY VANBALEN HOLT, *A DWELLING PLACE WITHIN*

2

Community

Where two or three are gathered in my name,
I am there among them.
MATTHEW 18:20

. . . so we, who are many, are one body in Christ
and individually we are members one of another.
ROMANS 12:5

HEN I WAS GROWING UP, eating was much more than just feeding our bodies. It was one of the only times our entire family was together. Many of my most vivid memories from childhood are of dinnertime. As I mentioned earlier, I am the eighth of ten children (all born within thirteen years) and dinnertime was sacred. We were always expected to make it home for dinner. We sat at a long picnic-style table with two benches on each side and my parents at each end. My father would go around the table and review everyone's day. If you didn't say more than "fine" he would ask the dreaded question: "So what new thing have you learned today"? We rarely answered "fine!"

There was a whole series of rules that we had to follow to keep order at the table. For example, when asking someone at the other end to pass the food, you had to immediately say, "No short stopping." This way the food was passed directly to you without anyone taking a scoop of it along the way. If, for some unfathomable reason, you forgot to say, "No short stopping," then each person between you and the food would take a scoop so that what finally arrived was an empty bowl.

There was also a definite pecking order as to who sat where. Sitting on "the crack" between the benches or on the end where you were in constant danger of being pinched or knocked off were places reserved for the youngest or most defenseless (anyone with a broken bone at the time) or for guests. Being a guest at our house was a little like going through fraternity hazing. But like a brotherhood, you were in for life—assuming you survived dinner.

Someone always had a friend or two visiting, so there were often guests at dinner. I was too young to remember, but my father loves to tell the story about when we all went sledding at a nearby park. We were all in red snow suits so we were easy to identify. At the end of a long day of sledding, my dad gathered all the red snow suits, loaded up the Volkswagen bus, and headed for home. About halfway through dinner someone asked who the extra kid was at the end of the table. Everyone assumed it was someone's friend but no one knew him. After a little work, they figured out who he was and how he came to be at our house—he was the new kid up the street and he had been wearing a red snow suit. My parents called his parents and offered to bring him right home but he refused; he was having too much fun at dinner.

vivid memories of dinner growing up

THE FAMILY TABLE has been our learning ground for all of our relationships. Being late to the table meant that we were being disrespectful to those who had taken time to prepare the meal. Each person was equal at the table; each one was given time to speak and be heard. We learned about each other; we empathized with the kid in the hot seat. As a parent now, I have tried to keep meal time a sacred time.

Unfortunately, the table where we come to share the eucharistic meal has lost the feeling of being a meal. It has become so ritualized that it has lost the essence of what it means to share a meal with each other. In the churches where I grew up, we weren't even allowed to let the host touch our teeth. Starting in the fourth century and culminating in the fifteenth, the laity was almost completely removed from participation in the eucharistic meal.

In the first century Christians celebrated Eucharist together. They shared a full common meal where each person brought what they could to share with the others. Paul reprimands the church for making distinctions within the community with some eating well and others not at all (1 Corinthians 11:19–22). It was important to retain the real substance of eating together and sharing everything they had.

The Second Vatican Council tried to bring us back to the essence of Eucharist as practiced in the early church by making the community a central element in the celebration. But the table of the Lord no longer looks like a table; we don't even call it a table—it's an altar. Our families would be stronger perhaps if we treated our dinner table more like an altar, symbolizing this sacred time, and our churches more vital if we became a family at the dinner table of the Lord.

In my work, I have found that people eat better in groups. My patients who are isolated in their hospital room often lose their appetite. The problem I have weaning them from tube feedings to oral feedings is more often due to poor appetite than due to physical disability. They may be on a modified diet and may need to remember to eat with precautions; but these are secondary issues.

My patients do better if they have family visiting during meals. It's best when friends or family bring in "home cooked" items and eat with them. Some patients will distract themselves with the TV or radio. Some even talk to themselves, but there is no substitute for another person. Eventually, they lose their appetite and even become depressed. Eating alone may feed the body but not the soul.

Similarly, I have seen children who have been tube fed from infancy who have great difficulty transitioning to eating by mouth. Everyone expects that they will just start eating when they are physically able, but it doesn't happen this way. These children haven't experienced mealtime in a normal way. They are hooked up to a tube that goes directly into their stomach and the "food" streams in from a bag hanging beside them. Eating by mouth for them is not only unusual, it's downright scary.

Sometimes, an elaborate sensory desensitization program and behavioral system is developed to reward them when they put food to their lips, then in their mouth, and finally when they swallow a bite. It can be a long arduous process. Many children don't start making the connection with eating by mouth until they are in a feeding group where they can see other children eating. When eating becomes part of the social activities of the day they no longer want to leave the group in order to receive the tube feeding. They watch the other children and start to experiment putting food in their mouth. Being part of the meal becomes important to them because it makes them part of the group.

Dinner table more like an alter
- Bless food
+ Being together
- light a candle - nice cloth
- Bible on table -
reading a book
- "Graces" - for meal
- Let children be children

I HAVE LEARNED that mealtime is a truly sacred time when we build bonds of intimacy with each other. If we look to the meal stories in scripture, we learn a great deal about community and family. There are a number of references to Jesus going off by himself to pray, but never to a time when he eats alone. Jesus uses mealtime or parables set around a meal to teach the fundamentals of faith and to describe the kingdom.

As I read these stories they all seem to deal with community in one way or another. To share a meal together is to be in solidarity with each other. The stories of feeding the multitude are rich in symbolism, which points to the importance of community. When Jesus was teaching the thousands gathered at Bethsaida he instructed the disciples to have the people recline in small groups—which parallels for me the experience of small faith communities or small churches within the larger universal church. They share what they have and God provides all with enough to eat, as he provided manna for the Israelites in the desert. The Israelites needed that time in the desert to become a community, a people of God.

During these meals there is always food left over, which shows there is always enough to welcome more people. In the story of the master's dinner party, he sends his servants out to gather the invited guests, but they excuse themselves from attending. The servants are then instructed to invite the poor and lame. The servants are continually asked to widen the circle of those who are invited. They report back again to the master that it has been done but there is still room. The master tells them to go out and find even more to invite because he says, "I want my house to be full." The kingdom banquet is for all of us and, as any large family knows, there is always enough for another place at the table.

And the symbols of community are not limited to the meal stories. Even the story of the crucifixion is a story of community. In the first century there were designated areas for the criminals to be crucified. Either a tree trunk or a sort of scaffolding was used with the vertical beam already in place. The convicted criminal would be forced to carry the horizontal beam ("the cross beam") on his back, through the town and up to the place of execution where he was then nailed to that beam. The horizontal beam was then pulled up and tied to the vertical beam, where he was also nailed.

When I read this for the first time it struck me that the vertical beam, which for me is symbolic of our individual relationship with God, is always there. It is the horizontal beam, the relationship we have with each other, that must be carried. Simon of Cyrene was pressed into service to help Jesus carry the cross to Golgotha. Although we are in fact too weak to carry our burdens, our sinfulness, our false selves, I don't think the central message is that Jesus was too weak to carry the cross alone, or that he will carry our cross for us. The central message for me is that we are not meant to carry our cross alone. Jesus showed us how to carry it with each other; he showed us the difficult task of accepting the help of the Spirit through others.

I believe that salvation does not come to us separately. I do not deny, in fact I am grateful for, a personal God, but I think we are saved together. Jesus tied the two commands together as if one flowed directly from the other, when he said that the greatest commandment was that we love God above all and our neighbor as ourselves. We can't answer "yes" to the question "Are you saved?" until we ask "Are my brother and my sister saved?" I think the reign of God will only come when enough of us are living as if we are saved—living dependent upon each other, accountable to each other, truly loving each other, being eucharist for each other.

The institutional churches try to convert us one at a time, but we need to be converted as community. Conversion doesn't happen in a vacuum—we are converted with and by each other. Metanoia occurs when we bump up against one another and are moved to change and grow. We are like diamonds in the rough. It's in the bumping and rubbing up against each other that God

Spiritual transformation or conversion

24

can chip away and polish our exterior. At the time it may feel like we are losing an important part of ourselves, but in fact, it reveals the diamond God created us to be.

The full community is the living Spirit. We are called to the cross and the table together. You can't have the kingdom banquet without community. There are no tables for one—we come together or there is no banquet.

> *We can take a lot of physical and even mental pain*
> *when we know that it truly makes us part of the life*
> *we live together in the world.*
> *But when we feel cut off from the human family,*
> *we quickly lose heart.*
> HENRI NOUWEN, *MAKING ALL THINGS NEW*

How do you connect this story w/ your small faith community

25

3

Service

[Jesus] got up from the table, took off his outer robe,
and tied a towel around himself.
Then he poured water into a basin
and began to wash the disciples' feet
and to wipe them with the towel that was tied around him.
After he had washed their feet, had put on his robe,
and had returned to the table,
he said to them, "Do you know what I have done to you?"
JOHN 13:4, 5, 12

I have learned so much about the human spirit by being involved in feeding and training others to feed. With the older folks, especially the men, I have seen how difficult it is for them to allow someone to feed them. They passively roll and move so the nurses can change their clothes, shave, or bathe them, but they almost always struggle for the fork. I have wondered about this for a long time. It seems so much more invasive and personal to have assistance going to the bathroom, or shaving. However, I have come to realize that giving someone food establishes a relationship. It is not just an exterior activity; this is now something that goes inside a person. It requires trust and a loss of control to accept food or drink from the hand of another.

As someone who values being in control, I can empathize with the anxiety resulting from a loss of control. When I see my patients struggle, I try to establish a relationship. I step back and try to get to know them a little better. I explain to them that their sensations and motor control will start to return and in the meantime I thank them for allowing me to feed them. I have learned about giving up control gracefully by watching them and I am amazed at their trust in me, a stranger.

When feeding patients, the feeder often stands looking down on the one being fed. For people with dysphagia, this puts them at risk of the food or liquid going down the wrong way. When the head is hyperextended (looking up) the airway is more open and it is more difficult for the larynx to rise and protect the airway during the swallow. Therefore, food or liquid is more likely to be aspirated. When I feed and when I train caregivers to feed, I have them sit down below eye level so that the head of the patient is in a natural chin-tucked position; this is usually the safest head position for swallowing.

IN JOHN'S GOSPEL the author doesn't describe the institution of the eucharistic meal with bread and wine; he describes the washing of the feet. Jesus gets down on his knees to show the disciples how they are to serve. He demonstrates for them the optimal position of service. I have often thought of this as I feed my patients. When you feed from above, "lording over them," you put the receiver at risk. It is dangerous for them to receive food in this position. It is when I put myself below the other person that they can then trust me and allow me to serve them. It's interesting that the optimal position for service puts the other person in the optimal position to receive.

During the Last Supper, Jesus and the apostles didn't sit down at a table that already had the food on their plate as we often do, each one feeding himself. The gospel says that Jesus broke the bread and gave it to them. And I suspect that they in turn gave it to each other. It would have been a very different atmosphere if it had been a banquet with waiters serving them at their place, each one eating independently.

You can sit down at a table or a lunch counter next to a stranger and eat independently of the other, never making physical or even eye contact. You can choose to interact or to remain strangers. But when you take food or a cup from someone's hand, you must make contact. When you make eye contact you become equals. When you accept the bread or cup, you accept each other. You are no longer strangers. The action of giving the bread and wine to the apostles bound them to Jesus and to one another. It demonstrated a personal, intimate relationship.

We also lose something when we make bread for Mass (or when we use a host) with no salt in the bread. In the first century salt was a precious commodity and was used sparingly. It is almost certain that salt was used in the unleavened bread, but more important for me is that salt was used as a symbol of relationship. Leviticus 2:13 and Numbers 18:19 talk of "a covenant of salt forever before the LORD." Job (6:6) was reduced to eating bread without salt as a sign of his destitution.

Aristotle quotes an ancient proverb which describes an intimate friendship by saying "they have eaten a bushel of salt together." How many meals it must take to share a whole bushel of salt! When we physically give Eucharist to each other as Jesus commanded, we establish a relationship with each other; we form community. And after having received Eucharist with each other over the course of our lives we might one day be able to say we have shared a bushel of salt with each other and with the Lord.

> *For who is greater, the one who is at the table*
> *or the one who serves?*
> *Is it not the one at the table?*
> *But I am among you as one who serves.*
> LUKE 22:27

4

Letting Go

Now his elder son was in the field;
and when he came and approached the house,
he heard music and dancing. . . .
Then he became angry and refused to go in.
His father came out and began to plead with him.
LUKE 15:25, 28

AMANDA WAS A BEAUTIFUL TODDLER with a mop of curly blond hair that was always falling in her face. She reminded me of Shirley Temple. She had a smile that competed with the brightness of the sun. She also had cerebral palsy. Specifically, ataxic CP, which means that, among other things, her motor movements came in fits and spurts and she had difficulty with balance.

When I first met Mandy she was two years old and moved around, as did many of our kids at the Cerebral Palsy Center, on a scooter board. It is a flat mat made of wood and four wheels. They would lie on their stomachs and push themselves around with their hands. Mandy was very good at scootering, but now at the age of four it was time for her to learn to walk with her leg braces. It would be a long and often painful process.

31

After many months of hard work, Mandy had learned to haltingly walk with the assistance of one of her teacher's fingers in each hand. Although she was capable of walking by herself she needed the assurance of that other person just in case she lost her balance. We all had been trying to convince her that she didn't need us to hold her up any more. We tried every reward. We tried bribery, flattery, and we told her she was a big girl and could do it on her own. Nothing could convince her to let go of our fingers.

One day her teacher had the brilliant idea of substituting her fingers for a daisy in each of Mandy's hands. They practiced walking short distances in the classroom for weeks and now Mandy was ready to leave the room and go to therapy all by herself. Mandy started to walk down the long hallway to my room. Her elbows were tight to her sides and her knuckles were white from gripping the daisies. She wore a worried look on her face but also the biggest smile she could manage.

Sitting at my desk I saw her coming so I squatted down to watch her. We were giddy with pride. As she came within five or six steps of me I reached out my arms ready to hug her when she arrived. To my surprise she stretched out her arms, opened her hands, let go of her daisies and slowly walked straight into my arms. I hugged her for a very long time.

To this day I don't think I have seen such courage. She was able to let go of the only thing that she thought was keeping her on her feet. She let go of her security to free her arms and hands to receive me. The hug of a friend was worth the risk.

AS I REFLECT ON MY OWN LIFE I wonder what are the false securities I hold on to and what would give me the strength and courage to let them go. I know that I hold on to the self-image of an overachiever, a rock, a problem solver. I'm afraid that if people, even those closest to me, see my faults and weaknesses they won't love me. There have been moments, though, when I have felt truly loved, when I was able to let go of my daisies and see myself as I was created. It is only in letting go that we become ready to open our arms and receive the love God has intended for us, and then know that we are children of God.

Edwina Gateley tells a story to the battered women that she works with. It goes something like this. There once was a country ruled by a king. The country was invaded and the king was killed, but the children were rescued by the servants and hidden away. An infant daughter was reared by some peasants. She became the farmer's daughter. She dug potatoes and lived in poverty.

Years later the young girl was in a field digging potatoes when an old woman appeared out of the forest and said to her, "Do you know who you are?"

"Yes" she said, "I am the farmer's daughter and a potato digger."

The old woman said, "No, you are the daughter of the king."

"I am?" she asked.

"Yes, that is who you are," answered the old woman who quickly disappeared into the forest.

The girl went on digging potatoes but she did it differently now. It was the way she held her head and the brightness in her eyes. For now she knew who she was. She was the daughter of the king. It is in letting go of the security of our own self-image and the image we accept from others, that we find out who we really are. We are children of the King.

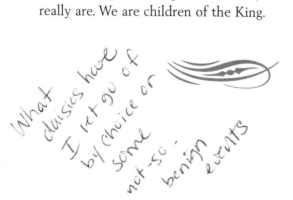

What daisies have I let go of by choice or some not-so benign events

WHEN JESUS GOES TO THE HOUSE of the Pharisee for a formal dinner, they had done everything right. They had set up the room and the table and they had dressed as would be expected of people of their station. Then a woman of ill repute barges in and kneels at the feet of Jesus. She washes his feet with her tears and dries them with her hair. The righteous guests and host are appalled that he would allow this to happen. Not only is this a woman in a place where only men were permitted, but she is also a woman with a very bad reputation. Doesn't Jesus know that you are judged by the company you keep?

In the first century it was understood that if you come in contact with someone who is unclean, it defiles you, it makes you unclean. In the story of the Good Samaritan (Luke 10:29–37), it is understandable that the priest and the Levite would walk by the man injured on the road because to stop and help could make them unclean. In this context, it is even more amazing that Jesus allows such a scandal. But Jesus is so secure in his Father's love for him, who he is in God, that he opens his arms and welcomes all people to himself.

Later, Jesus tells a parable of a great banquet being held by a father in honor of his wayward son. The father throws a huge party so that all may rejoice with him because his son has seen the light and returned home. But for most of my life I have identified more with the older brother. He is resentful that, after working so hard and doing all that is expected, his father doesn't throw the party for him. Even though he has been enjoying the home, the love and the devotion of his father all of his life, the elder brother feels cheated and hurt.

The sad part of the story for me comes (Luke 15:25–28) when the elder son hears the music and dancing but refuses to go in. Even after his father begs him, we are left to wonder if he could let go of his hurt, resentment, pride, and self-righteousness. I wonder how many of us will hear the music and dancing at the kingdom banquet but refuse to go in because it will mean that we must first give up our resentments, self-righteousness, prejudices, judgments, or image.

Many of us hold on to our judgments and what we think are societal expectations so we are not open to see that we are all the image of God. These are our daisies, our false securities. The real blessing is that if we can break through and see ourselves with true dignity, which only comes to us as children of God, we then are able to let go. And if we have the courage to let go of our daisies, our arms will be free to be received into the arms of our Lord.

> *Is there any chance for me to return to the Father*
> *and feel welcome in his home?*
> *Or am I so ensnared in my own self-righteous complaints*
> *that I am doomed, against my own desire*
> *to remain outside of the house,*
> *wallowing in my anger and resentment.*
> HENRI NOUWEN, *THE RETURN OF THE PRODIGAL SON*

complaint that kept me outside the house &

What would it take to let go of it?

What might happen if I did let go?

5

Gratitude

Give thanks in all circumstances;
for this is the will of God in Christ Jesus for you.
1 THESSALONIANS 5:18

Gratitude is the ability to experience life in a new way.
ROBERT WICKS, *STREET SPIRITUALITY*

THERE ARE TIMES when I can diagnose and treat a swallowing problem without much difficulty—it's a quick fix. I love them. Everyone thinks I've done something wonderful and miraculous. A mother brought in her infant because she was refusing to drink from her bottle. The infant girl was only a week old and was losing weight; the condition is called "failure to thrive." She presented her to the ER and they were deciding whether to admit her and start tube feedings or to hydrate her with an IV. They called me just in case there might be a swallowing problem.

The patient was small and skinny and had been a few weeks premature at birth. I watched mom feed her and noticed that after a few sucks she would pull away and push the formula out of her mouth. Mom said that they fight like this for about an ounce and then her baby stops sucking completely. It was evident to me that the infant was immature and overwhelmed. The formula was coming out too quickly for her. She didn't have time to swallow and breathe. It's a very common problem with premature infants.

After a short rest period, I asked the mom to try a low-flow nipple that I happened to have with me and to hold her child in an upright position to make it easier for her to swallow. She did those few simple things. The baby took a few ounces and happily fell asleep. Mom and baby went home happy, the doctors were happy, and they all thought I had just hung the moon. It's easy to be grateful on those days. But I am trying also to be grateful for those days when it seems that every room I leave I do so knowing that there is nothing I can do to fix the problem. These are the days when I feel most out of control. I think that if I only knew more, I could fix the problem.

There are times and patients that for one reason or another are beyond my capability. I had a student that I was training and she came to me very upset because she had just had a day like this—it would not be her last. She asked me how I handled feeling so helpless. I pray, I told her. It's a comfort to me that my patients are, in the end, in the hands of someone far greater than myself and so I leave the room putting them in God's hands. But it's still hard.

I am trying to learn to be grateful for these days because it reminds me that I am an instrument. It helps me keep perspective and it keeps me going back to God.

MY FATHER AND SOME OF THE PHYSICIANS I know have said that I should have been a doctor, that doctors have more power and control. But being a therapist has kept me in a position of assisting and not controlling. As a therapist, I make my recommendations to the physician and he or she decides whether or not to follow them. If I had any doubt at all about how little control I have, it became immediately clear to me when I became a parent. As they say, my life was no longer my own. Now with two teenagers in the house, my house and car are no longer mine either.

My mother used to say "give thanks in all situations." Being Catholic, I didn't realize that this was from scripture (1 Thessalonians. 5:18). I think gratitude unlocks the door to God because it opens the soul to the reality behind the present situation. It forces me to be patient, humble, and not in control. I never understood why some of the great saints like Francis and Therese of Lisieux would pray for humiliations. I think now that it must be because of the realization that whatever happens it is not of your doing. You can then see clearly the hand of God. Be ever present in gratitude and you'll be ever present to God.

*The discipline of gratitude is the explicit effort
to acknowledge that all I am and have
is given to me as a gift of love,
a gift to be celebrated with joy.*
HENRI NOUWEN, *THE INNER VOICE OF LOVE*

6

Grace

*. . . and hope does not disappoint us,
because God's love has been poured into our hearts
through the Holy Spirit that has been given to us.*
ROMANS 5:5

GOING FROM ONE PATIENT who entered the world a day or two ago to another who is ready to leave, has allowed me at times to see the bigger picture. I have seen infants born at twenty-four weeks who not only survive but also thrive. On the other hand, I work with families who carry the wounds brought about by living with handicaps, illness, and death. It has allowed me to see the cycle of life and many other patterns.

At the same time, the inexplicable miracles and tragedies have humbled me. I know that I am only seeing a glimpse of the whole pattern. For example, during my first year working at the hospital I had a patient who suffered a massive stroke and was not expected to live. He was awake for brief periods of time but was unable to move, to communicate or even swallow his own saliva. The family was prepared for the worst. When I returned the next day he was up walking and talking, and he had had breakfast with his wife and daughter. It was inexplicable but of course a very joyous occasion. Everyone said it was a miracle.

Less than a day later he died. It was not another stroke or any other event, just death. I felt angry and upset—how cruel to have their hopes so high only to have them crushed completely. The family was in shock and confused. Since then, I have seen this happen a few more times and I realize that it is a gift. At first it was disguised as tragedy, but looking at the bigger picture I see that it was grace. It is an opportunity that many don't get, to say their goodbyes. Although I have not been with the families, I believe that after the shock and sadness begin to diminish, they must be grateful for the time they were given and see that it was grace.

JESUS TEACHES USING STORIES AND PARABLES that are rooted in the patterns of everyday life. He shows us how to recognize God, and he describes the kingdom using everyday images. Jesus uses the things that every fisherman would know about when he speaks to Peter. Most people understand when Jesus speaks of faith being like a mustard seed because they live off the land. Many of his listeners are tenant farmers, and so his stories deal with debt and landlords. They also know when and where to plant their seeds and about the work involved in the harvest. Jesus tells them to "read the signs of the times" because they know how to predict the weather by reading the clouds.

Learning about the fisherman, the shepherd, and the farmer of the first century has brought depth and texture to the scriptures for me. Jesus doesn't use the Hebrew scripture as often as he uses nature, and human nature, to describe the kingdom and the love of the Father. Jesus used the everyday activities of work, parenting, paying the bills and eating together in part because this was practical and effective in a society where few people could read. Oral tradition was the primary method of conveying information.

Stories of everyday life were easier to remember and retell, but I think there was another reason. The deeper message is that God is infused in all the aspects of our lives. His word is written on our lives. I believe that our stories are gospel stories. If we never read scripture but were attentive to God in and around us, we could know Him. Scripture is God's revelation but the world and we, are also His revelations. Richard Rohr says it this way—"life is not about you, you are about life."

Other patterns can be seen in the way children learn. If you have ever watched a toddler learn to talk you will have seen it. Infants babble and coo, playing with volume and rhythm. Then they go through a stage called "jargon." At around nine to twelve months, before they really start using words and stringing them together, they talk in full paragraphs but it sounds like nonsense. They use rising intonation and a questioning look on their face but you don't know what they are asking. Or they fist their hands and say "words" with a strong downward inflection demanding something. At times they get very frustrated when you don't seem to understand what they are so obviously saying.

Children learn the rhythm of language before they learn the words. And before we hear and understand the Word of God we must be attuned to His voice. We need to feel the rhythms and watch for the patterns. Often it is only then that we can see the hand of God. I think that when we have ears to hear and eyes to truly see then we will recognize God's ever-present grace.

Some people say "there must be a God" when they see a tree or a sunset or a winning lottery ticket. Others find Him in solitude and silence. Some find Him in the voice of a loved one or in the eyes of a child. I would say that God is in the universal patterns of things no matter how small. This also means that He is present in all things and in all times. Even on days when I am feeling doubtful, I will hold an infant to feed him, I look carefully at the shape of the mouth, and I know that I will see God.

The shape of a child's mouth is especially meaningful to me because of a story told to me years ago by a plastic surgeon I'd met. Over the years our paths had crossed a number of times. He did reconstructive surgery on children with cleft palates and cleft lips. I would see the same children for feeding difficulties. I complimented him on the lip repairs he had done—they were the best I'd ever seen. He told me that he always took special care when reconstructing the "cupid's bow." The outline of the upper lip is called a cupid's bow because it is shaped like the handle of an archer's bow with a notch in the middle just under the nose.

This is the story the surgeon told me: before our souls are born into this world we trust completely, feel loved unconditionally, we understand all the mysteries of life and death because we are with God. Then just before birth God presses his finger to our lip and says "ssshhhh." Our mission is to rediscover what the newborn knows. God is in all things and in all times. Grace is the gift of God himself. In Mark's gospel, during the second multiplication of the loaves story, Jesus takes pity on the crowd saying "if I send them home hungry they will collapse on the way. . ." (Mark 8:3). Jesus knows that on our journey to discipleship we need nourishment or we will collapse on the way. God gives Himself to us as daily bread for the journey and that is grace.

The ordinary stuff of everyday living
is the stuff of which divine revelation is made.
BILL HUEBSCH, *A NEW LOOK AT GRACE*

1

The Call

[Jesus] saw Simon and his brother Andrew
casting a net into the sea—for they were fishermen.
And Jesus said to them, "Follow me
and I will make you fish for people."
And immediately they left their nets and followed him.
MARK 1:16–18

TEACH A CLASS in pediatric feeding and swallowing and often students will come to the hospital to observe. Even the very good students who have done all the reading and know the anatomy and physiology still find diagnostics difficult. It is especially difficult when feeding infants. Infants can't describe how it feels; they don't verbally complain; their symptoms can vary from moment to moment. Evaluating an infant means evaluating a dynamic, developing system, so "normal" also varies from week to week, even day to day.

I tell my students that a good diagnostician needs to be able to see things from different perspectives, to think outside the box—she can't assume if A then B. I use the optical illusion pictures to make the point. There is one with silhouette faces of two people facing each other almost nose to nose. If you look at the white space in between the faces you can see a vase or cup. Most of us see the faces first but can see the vase when it is pointed out to us. With some practice you can see both images at the same time. As I started reading the familiar scripture story about the meal at the house of Levi I decided I would try to read it from a different perspective, like a diagnostician.

I have read the story often but today I realized that I skip over the first part. I really start paying attention when Jesus says he will eat at Levi's house. But before the meal there is the call. I realize that I have done the same thing when I read about the call of James and John, Andrew, and Peter. They all left family, jobs, and lifestyle to follow this man named Jesus. Zebedee's sons just left their father there in the boat—they didn't even finish the day's work. I think I've dismissed the "call" portion of the stories because they seem so unrealistic.

My husband will tell you that I can be as spontaneous as the next person, just give me a week to plan it. Who in their right mind would leave everything behind? It must just be poetic license, or it makes the story more efficient. It could easily be considered irresponsible to abandon family and job to run off with some relative unknown, even if it did seem to be a good cause. It couldn't really have happened that way.

But what if it did happen just that way? The immediacy of the response may be incredible but I think it is only to point out the drastic nature of the call. It was a call to break completely with the system they knew. After letting this possibility sink in I then must ask myself the natural question—what would I do if I were called in such a manner? What would I do if I were asked to break completely from the system I took for granted, to see things from a completely new perspective? My reaction is a sigh of relief that I will never be asked this question.

As I read about the call of Levi again, I realize that unfortunately I have been asked to do just this. I have been called to leave many of the ideals and values held by much of my family, my neighborhood, and my society to follow the ideals and values of the kingdom.

WE HAVE ALL, AS A SOCIETY, agreed on the definition of success, love, and responsibility. We believe in the free market system, the myth of redemptive violence, and in love—unless it gets difficult. We believe that it is our responsibility to make as much money as possible to give our children the best of everything. To have enough in the bank so we are not a burden to our families or to society. We believe that there is a time and place for violence, that violence can be justified. We believe that people will make it on their own if they are forced to do so. We believe that a relationship should be evaluated on the basis of "if it makes us feel good." I think that when Jesus called the apostles he was asking them—and is asking us—to put all of our assumptions into question.

Many of our basic cultural assumptions and values are completely opposed to those of the kingdom. The first commandment is to have no other gods. But I am living immersed in a world that has so many potential idols. The idols of money, power, and especially of self. I was raised with a strong work ethic. Words like self-reliance, independence, self-determination, self-sufficiency are all signs that point to success. What they all have in common though is the "self" as the center. There is no room to be powerless and dependent on God. I struggle with balancing my ideas of being a competent, responsible person and provider for my family with true dependence on God. It's so easy to say that God is the Lord of my life but how can He be if I imagine myself so completely self-reliant.

Society's very definition of success seems to be in conflict with that of the kingdom. Success is measured in dollars and objects. Is it really God's ideal that we are totally independent of each other and not a burden? It seems that Jesus' description of the kingdom is where we take care of each other and welcome interdependency. My sister once said to my parents that the most valuable inheritance they will leave to the ten of us is that we will have each other. Jesus tells us: "Do not store up for yourselves treasures on earth" (Matthew 6:19). He tells us that we must be dependent on God for our daily bread and other basic needs. In one parable after another Jesus speaks of the danger of material attachments. Yet our culture tells us that we are not being responsible if we do not give our children a beautiful house, the best schools, extracurricular activities, and a head start.

I must ask myself: Is this living a simple lifestyle? With all this distraction can I possibly be teaching my children that only God is the God of our lives? If we are so prepared for the future and so invested in our present level of comfort, will we be free to seek out and see the will of God for us? Would success in God's eyes look the same as success in society's eyes?

IT'S FAIRLY UNIVERSALLY BELIEVED that violence is justified if there is a good and righteous cause. We of course decide what is righteous. We have justified wars, the death penalty, and vigilantism. But Jesus taught a doctrine of aggressive nonviolence. I don't recall one time when Jesus said, "Well, okay, you can kill under those circumstances." The myth of redemptive violence holds that violence can bring about peace. And at least in the short term it seems to work. But even when violence succeeds in defeating a horrible dictator or some other evil, the mere success of using violence teaches that violence is a viable and effective option and therefore perpetuates more violence. Walter Wink and others say that Jesus did not use the way of fight or flight but taught us an aggressive nonviolence as a "Third Way." It is a way to allow the creativity of God to intervene. Wink uses Jesus' teaching of turning the other cheek as one example. At first glance it appears that Jesus is telling us to be passive and just take the hit, even if it is unjust. Wink explains that in the culture of the first century it was a dehumanizing gesture to hit someone with the back of the hand. Using the palm of the hand was reserved for challenging a person of equal status. To turn the other cheek forced them to use the palm of the hand. In effect this made them equals.

The Third Way would allow both sides to regain and/or maintain their human dignity. This is not the way of the coward. In fact, I believe you could only follow this way out of great courage and faith, as it will inevitably lead to martyrdom. For me this is a very difficult way to even imagine. But it seems to be the way of Ghandi, Martin Luther King, and Jesus.

In trying to break from the values of society, which I think conflict with the values of Christ (even in small ways), I often feel that I am acting irresponsibly. I am reminded frequently that my choice of profession has severely limited my income earning potential. Our choices to drive older cars, not buy our children designer clothes, and minimize our debt are not choices upheld by much of society. If I can't afford to send my children to the best college or worse yet, make them pay for college themselves, I feel like a bad parent.

People speak of the limited choices of the poor, but we are bound also by image, convention, and societal expectations. We are bound and don't even recognize it. I wonder if it's even possible to get away from the "more is better" mentality. Even with good motivations I see how much I am influenced by it.

I always wanted to serve others but not just a few. I wanted my mission in life to be big and important. I'd like to cure cancer, bring peace to the world, or eliminate starvation.

Instead, my life's work is to feed the relatively few that are brought my way. This is a blessing for me because it reminds me to try to live by the words of Mother Teresa. She said: "We cannot do great things—only small things with great love." This is the view of life to which I need to aspire.

What I have tried to teach my children is to be kind and generous; to be forgiving and to accept forgiveness from others; to be joyful and mostly to know that there is a great God who loves them. We play a game after prayers at night. After we finish we go back and forth saying "I love you" and "I love you more." But then I say, "who loves you most?" and they say "God." I ask "Why" and they say, "Because He can." It may seem like a silly routine but I hope they will always know deep inside of them that beyond everything else they can find their security in knowing a loving God.

The church teaches us to avoid the three P's (power, prestige, and possessions) because they are the primary idols or false gods. Society measures success by the same three P's. I think that Jesus is calling me in the same drastic, unrealistic way that he called the apostles. He asks that my power, prestige, and possessions lie solely in him, that I find my security in him. He asks me to believe that I am his beloved. He asks me to see life from a new perspective, which inevitably leads me to look at my lifestyle from a new perspective as well. I must admit my fear that if Jesus challenged me as he did the young rich man, that I too might walk away sad.

As Jesus was walking along,
he saw a man called Matthew sitting at the tax booth;
and he said to him, "Follow me."
And he got up and followed him.
MATTHEW 9:9

8

Prayer and Action

*Immediately he made his disciples get into the boat
and go on ahead to the other side, to Bethsaida,
while he dismissed the crowd.
After saying farewell to them,
he went up on the mountain to pray.*

MARK 6:45–46

I OFTEN HAVE DIFFICULTY balancing the different aspects of my life. But today, one of my infant patients taught me a lesson. Baby William is thirty-two weeks gestational age and weighs about two and a half pounds. I decrease all the stimulation around him as I swaddle him and take him out of the incubator for his first bottle-feeding. I position him so I can watch his face. I listen for aspiration and breathing patterns with my stethoscope to his neck. My right hand holds him on his upper back and head so I can position his head and feel him breathe. He is nestled in the triangle of one of my legs crossed over the other. I try to block out all the other stimulation so he can concentrate on feeding, which is his most complex motor task.

As I feed baby William I count his sucking bursts and pauses. His pattern is three suck-swallows, then seven breaths. After a few tries he stabilizes. He finds his pattern, three then seven, three then seven. The breath comes late this time. I wait with him, holding my breath too. I don't want to stimulate him too soon. He needs to self-regulate, to take that breath on his own, if he can. I'll be there with a little squeeze on his back if he needs a gentle reminder. "Breathe, little one," I say to him in my mind, "breathe."

I'm not sure how I know when to wait for another second or when to give that little nudge. Something just tells me he needs help or that this time he'll do it on his own. With William I can feel my own breathing waiting for his. William gets stuck. I call it the "deer in the headlights" reaction. He has too much to do. He has to breathe but there is fluid in this throat so he needs to swallow first but to swallow he needs to suck, which will give him more fluid. He can't do it all so he stops completely. I tip the bottle down and prompt an empty suck so he can swallow. Then I blow a small puff of air in his face, which gently startles him and he starts to breathe. I whisper to William, "breathe, for now, just breathe." He takes his breath and pants for a few seconds then starts to calm.

Premature infants often go back to sucking when they are still panting, needing air. Often, I need to hold them back and impose a longer rest period between sucking bursts. Only when they have calmed can they successfully go back to work. My work and my rest also have a pattern. It's like the mantra of my life. I need to keep this rhythm. If I forget to breathe, to break and be with the holy breath that feeds me, my Father will wait for a while hoping I will remember on my own to come back to him. But if I forget he will give me a squeeze to remind me that I need him. I need to pause longer, to not go back to work until I am really ready. I need to wait until I'm filled; only then can I go back to work again. So often the Lord must remind me: "Breathe, for now, just breathe."

THE STORY OF JESUS' VISIT to Martha and Mary is also about balance. In Luke's gospel it comes at the end of a section on prayer including when Jesus teaches us how to pray. The Martha story teaches us about the balance between prayer and action, discipleship and ministry. I am a Martha. I like to do. We are a society of doers. I have been a doer at work, at home, and at church for as long as I can remember. At times I have been so out of balance that I forget who's in charge.

I remember in college being on a retreat and pouring out my heart to the spiritual director about all the hardships I was having with my various ministries. I told her that I didn't have enough volunteers to participate in the social ministries I was organizing; the liturgy committee felt stale; some of our prayer groups were breaking up. I went on and on about all the things I was doing to fix everything but nothing seemed to be working. Finally, she stopped me and said: "I didn't realize God was looking for a replacement."

Martha is the patron saint of all of us doers. Can you imagine how distracted you might be if the bishop or the pope were coming to dinner. It's that busyness to distraction that Jesus has to startle her out of by saying, "Martha, Martha."

There are other times when God uses a name twice. For example when he calls Samuel out of his sleep (1 Samuel 3:10); or when Jesus confronts Peter at the Last Supper (Luke 22:31); or Saul on the road to Damascus (Acts 9:4). In each case it is an announcement, a call to attention for us all. He's saying "Listen, this is important." Jesus doesn't respond to Martha's complaint,

He responds to the real problem, that Martha is distracted from a relationship with God, which is what gives meaning to the rest of life. He tells Martha that Mary has chosen the better way. Mary chose the way of true discipleship. She knew that first she must sit at the feet of Jesus and listen before going out to serve.

Henri Nouwen, in his book *Out of Solitude* (Ave Maria Press, 1984) reminds us that "we are worth more than the result of our efforts" and that "our worth is not the same as our usefulness." Jesus molded the balance between prayer and action for us in many ways (Luke 5:16; Mark 6:46; Luke 6:12; Luke 22:41). In Mark 1:32–39, Jesus is healing, preaching, and casting out demons, but in the middle of this exciting story the author writes: "In the morning, while it was still very dark, he got up and went out to a deserted place, and there he prayed."

It is only when I have taken the time to be in silence and solitude with the Lord that I start to see life with new eyes. I allow God to regain control and I am finally again at peace. I become more attentive to the moments of grace that fill my day. In prayer, I am reminded that grace, that relationship with the Father, is freely given. It's already out there. I can't work to make it happen or make myself worthy of it. I must just be open to receive it.

My need for balance was, at least in part, what attracted me to Buddhism as a young adult. Looking back I know some of the attraction was the elements of the mystical, universal union, and just being in the presence of something inexplicable and incomprehensible. My personality is much more biased toward the concrete, sensible, and definable. I think I was craving a place where I could meet something greater than myself, a place to be rather than do.

I continue to crave that place of grace. I know for myself that I am far less likely to recognize the action of grace in my life when I am like Martha, distracted by many things. There are times, and they are all too frequent, when I am caught up doing things, controlling things. Most of the time my motives are good. I'm doing things for others. But then I am doing the work *for* God instead of the work *of* God. When I go back to silence and solitude God shows me that I can trust him and there he feeds me.

But now more than ever
the word about Jesus spread abroad;
many crowds would gather to hear him
and to be cured of their diseases.
But he would withdraw to deserted places and pray.
LUKE 5:15–16

9

Sacrament

The words that I say to you I do not speak on my own;
but the Father who dwells in me does his works.
JOHN 14:10

Sacraments are the celebration
of the presence of Christ in our midst.
THOMAS RICHSTATTER, O.F.M., *CATHOLIC UPDATE*

HE WORDS *SACRED, SACRIFICE,* AND *SACRAMENT* all have the same root word in Greek meaning "holy mystery," or in the verb form "to make holy." In scripture it connotes a mystery, which shows God's saving presence. I was taught as a child that a sacrament was "an outward sign of inward grace," and grace was defined as "a divine action or encounter." All of the great religions use symbols to mark and ritualize moments of divine encounter.

The foundations for our sacraments came from the Hebrew scriptures and Jewish traditions. These traditions include an official confessional rite since the time of Solomon, Rabbis anointing the sick with oil, and of course John the Baptist calling Jews to repentance and renewal (Luke 3:3). We have carried on this sacramental tradition. The church developed the major sacraments to mark important points on the faith journey based on the life of Jesus and the early church. The baptism of Jesus was of course the basis of our Rite of Baptism (Mark 1:9–11).

There were many anointings. Jesus points out to the Pharisee that a woman anointed his feet with her tears and perfume (Luke 7:37–39). To the dismay of Judas, Jesus allowed the anointing of his head with precious oil, which we continue doing today during our rites of initiation and confirmation. The early church sent people forth in ministry by laying hands on them (Acts 6:6). And although I think he was ritualizing the presence of God in all the meals, Christ instituted our central sacrament of Eucharist during the Last Supper.

Our sacraments are bonded to everyday things and actions like water and cleansing, precious oils and the human touch, food and eating together. These symbols elicit a visceral reaction. We know what they mean in our bones. If God only presented himself in the extraordinary then our choice of symbols would be objects or actions that would also be extraordinary. God chose to use the ordinary so that we could see his presence in all things, including our own lives. Our lives don't have to be extraordinary to feel and express God's presence. The way we relate to one another, sacrifice our time or energy or material goods for each other, give freely of our love and ourselves—these are the sacraments of life.

Through time, however, the holy mystery of God's grace was reduced to measurable behaviors. There was no Eucharist unless the exact words of institution were said by someone with the authority to say them and for the most part the laity no longer participated in the meal.

Our phraseology gave us away; priests administered sacraments; they heard confessions and distributed communion. Man could now manipulate God's grace with the right words and gestures. The sacraments became distant from the daily activities in which they were rooted. The Second Vatican

Council helped us to bind the ritual back to the actual when it stated that symbols and actions used in the sacraments should be more like the actual event that they symbolize. But I think many still feel that God only touches their lives during the sacraments, which is when they can *store up* grace.

The sacraments were intended to be signs of personal contact with the divine but this contact is not intended to be limited to five or six times in our lives. I see the seven major sacraments like mile markers on our journey. They are like the chapter titles, but the substance, the meat of the story, is within the pages of each chapter. The wedding, for example, is the celebration of the sacrament of marriage. But the sacrament itself is celebrated in the daily loving relationship shared by two people. God doesn't just visit us once and again within the context of a ritual. Each day is infused with grace as God tries to pursue us.

MR. JONES was in the renal care unit. He had been deaf for many years and so he primarily used sign language. He was referred to me for swallow therapy and to help him communicate with the staff. Mr. Jones was in his seventies and in multiorgan failure. When we met he had a breathing tube in his throat; he was on a ventilator at night and on kidney dialysis three to five times a week. At least two acts of grace brought us together. I knew sign language but was not a family member (making it easier for him to talk to me). I also had a light caseload, which was unusual for that time of year but it gave me more time to spend with him.

After a few weeks, we became friends. Unfortunately, therapy for his swallowing was not successful and a feeding tube was placed into his stomach. He knew he was terminal. He was in a great deal of pain and was ready to stop the many invasive procedures and to allow death to come to him. I knew he could sign the papers and go to comfort care measures at any time. I never knew him to complain. He was always willing to wait while the nurses took care of someone else first—in fact, he insisted upon it. He always asked me how my day was going. His daughter told me that he was the heart of their family. He was the glue that held them together.

One day when he was more tired and worn than usual, I asked him why he was holding on. He told me that his family was not ready to let him go. He explained that he needed to be here and help them through their grief. He said he would know when the time was right and then he would be free to go. Every day we talked and we laughed a lot. At less than a hundred twenty pounds, his body was feeble but he still had an incredibly strong spirit.

One Friday when I walked in, Mr. Jones looked joyous and peaceful. He signed to me with great animation, "My family is ready." He had been in the ICU six months now since the day I met him. He had told his physician to stop dialysis and the ventilator support. We talked for a while longer and then I kissed him good-bye. I knew he would be gone when I got back on Monday. Mr. Jones taught me the meaning of sacrifice. He had made his life and the very process of his death sacred, an outward sign of inward grace.

Our very lives are holy mysteries. Our lives present a facet of the divine to the world. Christ offered himself to us, showing us that unconditional love of God. He ritualized this reality in the simple act of eating together. He asked us to continue the practice so we would remember the love that it symbolizes. From the earliest time, Eucharist was shared daily. Jesus teaches us to pray "[G]ive us this day our daily bread. . . ." This reminds me that I must go back to God each day, not just on special occasions. I can't get away from God.

For me, sacrament is a way of life instead a marker of life's events. We are called to live the holy mystery that Jesus showed us how to live. We are called to die and sometimes live for each other. We are called to make our lives sacramental, an outward sign of inward grace.

All of these are symbols—
the other world keeps coming into this world.
Like cream hidden in the soul of milk,
No-place keeps coming into place.
Like intellect concealed in blood and skin,
the Traceless keeps entering into traces.
And from beyond the intellect,
beautiful Love comes dragging its skirts,
a cup of wine in its hand.
And from beyond Love, that indescribable One
who can only be called THAT keeps coming.
JALALUDDIN RUMI, *THE SUFI PATH OF LOVE*

O God of light, love, the ordinary + the extraordinary.

Hear our prayers that we have lifted up to you tonight. Thank for this time together which you have given us. Help us to see your presence in our everyday lives and help us be more Christ-like as we carry out our roles + responsibilities. Continue to be with us when we're up on the mountain, down in whether the valley, or just walking along.

AMEN

10

Whose Plan?

Man makes his plans to be often upset by God.
But at the same time,
where the ultimate goal is the search for truth,
no matter how a man's plans are frustrated
the result is never injurious
and often better than anticipated.

GHANDI

HEN THE INFANTS ARE BIG ENOUGH and healthy enough, they are moved from the intensive care unit to a step down unit. There the babies have time to develop and grow. At this stage they are called "feeder growers" because this is now the major task. They need to bottle feed or breast feed well enough to accommodate their physiological needs and to grow before they are ready to go home. Right now the nursery seems full of feeder growers who won't feed or grow.

The parents have spent weeks or months on a roller coaster visiting their children in the ICU where the status of their child changes day to day, even hour to hour. They endure cycles of fear and relief, experiencing one medical complication after the next and then some measure of recovery. Many parents have told me that in some ways this time of waiting becomes the most difficult. After the major traumas are over, they are ready to take their baby home—now. Each parent today wanted to know exactly when that day would come.

It's a question I can't answer. I completely understand their need to know. There are so many plans to make. When should the grandparents visit? When should we take off from work? Is the nursery ready? I try to reassure them that the day will be here soon but that each child is different and we can't make definite plans. Our job is to facilitate the infants' development, but they have their own timetable. If we try to force a plan, they invariably won't cooperate. It's time to wait and watch. The parents try so hard to be patient and to accept the uncertainty, but we all know how difficult it is for them and wish that we could make it easier by giving them a definite plan.

IT IS A COMFORT to me that even Jesus had plans that didn't work out quite the way he expected. The wedding at Cana is one example and has always been a favorite of mine. One reason I like this story is because the relationship between Jesus and Mary seems so real, so typical. It's one of only a few times when we see Jesus and Mary interact. The other familiar time is when Joseph and Mary have been looking for their young son, Jesus, for three days and they find him in the temple. Jesus is amazed that they are so worried about him. He had a plan and wondered why it was so upsetting to his parents.

Scholars have speculated why we don't hear about Jesus' life from that time until he started his ministry. I don't wonder about it at all. I can hear the conversation between Mary and

Jesus as they walked all the way back to the caravan after finding him that day. Jesus says: "Didn't you figure out that I'd stay and talk to the scholars in the temple and be with my Father?"

Mary replies naturally: "You're grounded until you're thirty!"

The next time we see Jesus isn't until the wedding at Cana. This encounter between Mary and Jesus unfolds a little differently. It is suggested that these newlyweds are part of Mary's extended family. Mary is concerned because the hosts are running out of wine. She knows that running out of wine would be seen as a breach of hospitality that would bring shame and dishonor to the family. She goes to Jesus, knowing he can fix this, and tells him to take care of it.

Jesus first tells her: "It's not my time; it's not the plan." He's referring to revealing himself with his first miracle, but Mary persists. Maybe she was just concerned about her friends and didn't want them to be embarrassed. Or maybe Mary knew that Jesus' disciples needed to be reassured in their decision to follow him ("[Jesus] revealed his glory; and his disciples believed in him" John 2:11). In the end Jesus obediently deferred to his mother's plan instead of his own.

I remember hearing this reading in church one Sunday and I was really disturbed by it. Jesus would certainly know God's plan for him and Mary shouldn't try to change God's plan. It may be maturity over the years or just my changing roles from young adult to parent but the story changed for me. I was no longer upset by Mary's interference. My belief in a divine plan for all of us has changed. At some point (I don't know when), I came to believe that God has the same plan for us—to get to know him and be in relationship with him.

I don't believe that we are to take a certain road in order to find him. I think that, like Jesus at the wedding, when we come to a decision or a cross road we make the best decision we can and God will walk that road with us, regardless. I have had too many parents ask: "Why did God make my child handicapped?" or "Why did he take my baby?" to believe that this is God's plan. I think awful things like disease, accidents, and death happen. Some tragedies are caused by poor decisions of another person and we all have to take responsibility for our part in the evil that seems so pervasive in this world. I don't believe that God makes bad things happen to good people as part of his plan.

I believe that God has the power and creativity and love to transform all of our tragedies into blessings. He proved this by taking the worst possible event, the killing of the God-man Jesus, and transforming it into the resurrection of the world. Saint Teresa of Avila said it this way: "God can write straight with our crooked lines." It is our job to be open to God, whatever road we choose to travel. Then we will be following God's plan.

God, without sparing us the partial deaths or the final death,
which form an essential part of our lives;
transfigures them by integrating them in a better plan,
provided we lovingly trust in Him.
TEILHARD DE CHARDIN

11

Gospel

The commandment we have from him is this:
Those who love God must love their brothers and sisters also.
1 JOHN 4:21

Then Jesus told his disciples,
"If any want to become my followers,
let them deny themselves
and take up their cross and follow me."
MATTHEW 16:24

THERE ARE SOME DAYS when it is more difficult than others to see the hand of God. Today was one of those days. It seemed as though so many of my patients were awful. Ms. Whitaker was screaming all night—she is an elderly woman with multiple medical problems, all relatively minor and none fatal. She has nursing aides around the clock at home and she doesn't want to do anything for herself. She knows she is capable and that she needs to be active or her muscles will continue to atrophy and cause her more pain and debilitation. It's a vicious cycle. Still, she complains if she is asked to do even the most basic tasks for herself. She is angry all the time. I suspect she has been angry for a very long time.

This morning when I went into the room she had been screaming for a few minutes because the nurse had to take care of her many other patients. I tried to explain this to Ms. Whitaker but she screamed all the louder. I tried to distract her by starting our therapy objectives for the day. She then took a swat at me. After the first few days of being hit, I've learned to lean back just in time to avoid her frail but accurate hand. That really makes her mad. I've tried cajoling and coddling, being firm and understanding, but without success. I'd like to discharge her; I can't get through to her.

From there I went to radiology to do a swallow study (an x-ray of swallow function) on Mr. Smith. Mr. Smith is in his mid-twenties and suffered a severe traumatic brain injury in a motorcycle accident about six years ago. He has a shunt in his head to drain fluid, which accumulates on his brain. He is in a wheelchair on his good days; otherwise his movements are limited to his bed. As is typical of severe traumatic brain injury, he has difficulty controlling his impulses. He often swears and will blurt out inappropriate things.

As we sat waiting for the test to begin, I noticed a tattoo on his arm and asked him what it meant. He proudly told me it was the symbol of the clan. I naively asked what clan and he said the Ku Klux Klan. He then added, "I just hate those nigras." I was grateful that at that very moment the radiologist walked in so I could hide my shock with the task at hand.

After the study I left the room for a few minutes to review the results. As I walked back in the room the radiology technician was in tears and hurriedly passed by me. She is a sweet woman in her thirties and she is black. I stopped to see what was wrong and she choked out "he urinated on me." I ran in to see Mr. Smith. I asked him if he had a problem controlling his bladder, did he know what he had done? He said "Damn right I did, I won't have those nigras touching me." I told him that what he did was inappropriate behavior; that she was there to help him and she was an employee of the hospital and must be treated with respect.

This obviously had no effect. The tech took care of reporting the incident to her department and I went back to the room with the patient, to file the incident report with the charge nurse. I then went to talk to his parents who are his caregivers. I was sure that they would be embarrassed by his behavior and reasoned that it must be at least in large part due to the characteristic impulsivity resulting from the head injury. I related the story to the parents and waited for their reaction.

They responded: "Well what did you expect him to do? They shouldn't be allowed to touch him." I could barely control my temper. I reiterated to them that they needed to be respectful of all his care providers. I was grateful that at this point it was out of my hands and into the hands of the administration.

And, as if this weren't enough, one of our infant patients was discharged today with her mother. But her mother has already lost three older children because of abuse or neglect. They can't take this child until there is evidence of abuse or neglect of this infant. So at five pounds, two ounces, this baby girl leaves today with only our hopes and prayers that her mom has changed and will take care of her.

LORD, I KNOW YOU TOLD US to love each other and I'm supposed to find your presence in everything, but I just don't like these people. I don't want to go back tomorrow and treat these patients. Some are nasty; others are downright hateful. The system doesn't defend those who need it most. Please change my heart. Help me care for these people.

In so many of the meal stories you brought a message of inclusion. You challenged the Pharisees to accept those they had judged to be sinners and unworthy. At the Last Supper you challenged your apostles to be servants of all. You tell us that in serving the least of our brothers we serve you. But I don't recognize you in these people. Teach me to let go of my anger and hatred.

I realize that it's anger and hatred that has eaten away at some of my patients. Help me to recognize myself in them and my own potential to be judgmental, egocentric, and demanding. Teach me to care for my brothers as if it was you. Your message continues to challenge me today. I know that I cannot profess to love you, Jesus, unless I am obedient to your word. But I'm going to need a lot of help on days like this one.

In the book *In the Steps of the Master* by H.V. Morton (Dodd Mead, 1984), the author takes us through the sites of the Holy Land, relaying stories of today and of the past. He says in describing the relics in the Church of the Holy Sepulchre that they were worn and almost entirely devoid of their original color after having been touched so often. He wisely observed that the effects of severe neglect and ardent adoration were the same. So even adoration or love can be as destructive as ignoring something completely. The adoration of relics can easily move into the realm of kneeling down before graven images.

I think that, in a way, even worship of the person of Jesus can distract us. Of course Jesus should be worshiped, in a sense, but not in order to ignore the message he came to bring. Jesus was forever pointing to the Father and describing the kingdom. Jesus said to follow him, not to stop at him. He showed us the way to move forward. At the transfiguration the disciples wanted to build a place on the mountain to stay and worship Jesus. But Jesus said, "No, you can't stay here; go down from the mountain and be changed."

Professing love of Jesus can't be a substitute for living the message he brought. He tried to teach the message of justice and love of God and neighbor through his word and example but we didn't get it. Either the message was too difficult to hear and understand because it so threatened our social structure or our self –image. Or in the other extreme (the zealots) it was fine that the message was countercultural and radical, even revolutionary, but it wasn't their concept of revolution.

I am ashamed to say it, but I can relate to Judas. I think he understood that Jesus was going to turn the world upside down. Jesus just wasn't going about it in the way Judas expected. Judas expected Jesus to lead a violent revolution and free them from oppression. I think when he handed Jesus over he was trying to force Jesus' hand. If he could push Jesus into a corner in front of the Sanhedrin he would reveal his true identity and the revolution would begin. Judas was completely successful. What he didn't recognize was that Jesus wasn't there to replace one political or social system with another; he was there to do away with them all and usher in the kingdom. It would be a violent revolution, but the victor would be the victim.

I, TOO, HAVE TRIED to force someone into action assuming my way was the right way. Worse yet, I have tried to force God's hand. Although the apostles loved Jesus, they all had difficulty understanding the message the way I do today. Even while adoring Jesus, they were blinded to the message, and in that sense they didn't really know Jesus. It's like when you first fall in love, you are smitten before you really know the person. Or when someone after years of marriage says, "Sometimes I don't think you even know me."

I wonder if Jesus felt this way when he lost his temper with Peter (Matthew 16:23), or when the disciples didn't recognize him on the road to Emmaus (Luke 24:13-35). Maybe this is what Jesus meant before when he said: "I am the good shepherd. I know my own and my own know me" (John 10:14). I have to ask myself, would I recognize him on the road? What needs to be broken and given away? What parts of me blind me from seeing or really knowing Jesus and his message? Am I ready to join the meal of Emmaus?

The disciples journeying to Emmaus did not recognize Jesus because they were not ready for the message and what it asked of them. They did not recognize what was now required of them. They needed to see that this story was not one where they were spectators or even narrators—watching Jesus, learning his theology and then telling others about it. This story required of them and requires of us that we become actors in the play. We must be participants. It's a hard message, this not making gods out of money, social status, intellect, image, or even church, and loving one another as he loves us—unconditionally.

The two on the road had left the city because they did not believe the women who came back from the tomb; they needed to see for themselves. But when given the opportunity the disciples still did not really see because they didn't really know Jesus. They came to know him in the breaking of the bread because they realized that they too must be broken and given up to others, for the sake of others. When finally they recognized the Lord they went back to Jerusalem to tell the others the good news. Even though it is a difficult message to live, in the end it was still good news—it was gospel.

We pray for messages from God, for signs and wonders, but they are here all the time so that we might recognize him. How many times have I looked upon the face of Jesus in one of my patients who are combative or angry and turn away to treat someone more cooperative? How many times have I missed the voice of God because I was too busy to listen to my children? Like the disciples of Emmaus, do I not recognize the face of Jesus?

If I recognize him, if I truly love him then I must follow his message. If I recognize him in the poor, I might have to give up my possessions and provide for them. If I recognize him in the wicked, I might have to give up my fear and my judgments and try to heal or comfort them. If I recognize Jesus in all things, I might have to examine all my choices. Recognition comes with a steep price. I would have to change. Maybe this is the cross I must bear—to continually let go of my attachments.

Robert Wicks says that we fill our arms with many little crosses. These little crosses carry names like fear, anger, hatred, self-righteousness, resentments, and hurts. He says we need to let go of these little crosses so that our arms are ready to carry the cross that God has intended for us.

I think Jesus had to mingle the message with his person so in loving him we would come to know the message. He had to literally become the message so when we adore him we must be changed by the message and finally follow him and be his disciples. Jesus came to show us the way through to the kingdom and how to live in the kingdom now. In the early church, before they were called Christians, they called themselves "people of the way." Not people of Jesus, but people of the way. The emphasis was on what Jesus came to teach us and what he taught us was how to be people of the way.

It is no use walking anywhere to preach
unless our walking is our preaching.
SAINT FRANCIS OF ASSISI

12

Forgiveness

Bear with one another and,
if anyone has a complaint against another,
forgive each other;
just as the Lord has forgiven you,
so you must also forgive.
COLOSSIANS 3:13

The weak can never forgive.
Forgiveness is the attribute of the strong.
GHANDI

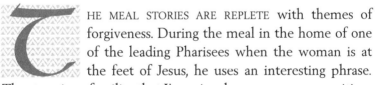HE MEAL STORIES ARE REPLETE with themes of forgiveness. During the meal in the home of one of the leading Pharisees when the woman is at the feet of Jesus, he uses an interesting phrase. The story is so familiar that I've missed my own presupposition. Jesus says that because she has been forgiven much she shows such great love. Forgiveness begets love, not the other way around. I assumed that God forgives us and we forgive each other because we love each other. If you love someone more you can probably forgive him or her more.

But Jesus says it's the feeling of being forgiven that opens us up to love. This kind of forgiveness is not begrudging. It must make the person being forgiven feel and know that they are in right relationship with us again. It's not to be used as a constant reminder with the spoken or unspoken words "because I forgave you then. . . ." This would not be forgiveness at all and it does not restore the relationship, but undermines it.

When Jesus appears to the disciples on the beach after the resurrection, he invites them to a meal of fish over a charcoal fire. There he asks Peter three times if he loves him. Peter repeatedly says: "Yes, Lord," but does not understand why Jesus would ask the same question over and over again. I think Peter needed to be restored to a right relationship not only with Jesus but also with himself. At a previous charcoal fire, Peter denied Jesus three times. Peter's denial was also a denial of himself, of who he truly was. Peter denied his identity as the friend of Jesus and a beloved son of God.

Even though I'm sure Peter knew that Jesus had forgiven him (even before it happened Jesus had predicted it and had already forgiven him), Peter needed to forgive himself and to be restored. Jesus allowed Peter to erase the previous three denials with three testimonies of love, replacing one charcoal fire with another and symbolizing the reunification with a shared meal.

In Matthew's gospel the primary function of the eucharistic meal seems to be forgiveness. At the Last Supper, Jesus says, "for this is my blood of the covenant, which is poured out for many for the forgiveness of sins" (Matthew 26:28). We are also told to leave our gifts at the altar and go first to be reconciled with our brother. It seems that if we are not in right relationship with one person, we cannot be in true union with our community. Our relationship with one affects our relationship to all.

I have found this to be true in my own life and in the lives of others. Even our relationship with ourself affects our relationship with others and the community. Mark adds emphasis to the Lord's Prayer: "If you forgive others their transgressions, your heavenly Father will forgive you. But if you do not forgive others, neither will your Father forgive your transgressions" (Mark 6:14–15). I don't think this statement is to force us to forgive under threat of eternal damnation. I think it is God's lesson to us that if we are not in right relationship with each other we cannot be in right relationship with God.

Lack of forgiveness holds both parties captive. When a person can't forgive, they cannot truly love. In order to hold on to the debt, we must hold on to and remind ourselves of the pain or anger the transgressor has caused us. We are called to forgive in all situations but not necessarily forget. There are times when it is healthy and proper to expel someone from your life because of his or her harmful behavior. You can forgive without putting yourself in unhealthy or dangerous positions. The more difficult times are those like Peter's, when we need to forgive ourselves.

I SPOKE TO A PATIENT'S DAUGHTER TODAY who seemed so angry with her mother. She was angry at the inconvenience of coming to the hospital. She didn't think her mother was really that sick. During the conversation it was obvious that she was angry at a myriad of things. I couldn't figure out the real problem. When I asked how things had been going at home with her mom, the daughter started to tear up and said, "Do you think I caused this?" Her tone wasn't accusatory, it was obvious that she was blaming herself for her mother's illness and lashing out at anything she could find, including her mother.

I reassured her that it was not her fault. She had been taking very good care of her mother; it was the unfortunate course of the disease. The relief was immediately apparent in her eyes and

I asked if she needed a hug. She said, "I'm afraid I do." We could talk then about what new things they might want to do at home to make eating safer, but mostly I continued to reassure her. It seems that this daughter was not free to love her mother until she had forgiven herself for her believed neglect.

A few years ago there was a similar situation in the neonatal intensive care unit (NICU). One of our mothers was not coming in to see her baby. She had had multiple medical problems during the pregnancy and the baby was born prematurely. No one seemed to know why only the dad was coming in to see the baby. One day when she did visit, she was very tearful. The baby was actually doing very well but the mom did not stay and didn't want to hold her child.

A week or two later she came in so I could teach her how to feed her baby. During the conversation she again became tearful and said very softly, "This is my fault." I realized that the reason she had difficulty visiting and loving her child was because she blamed herself for the premature birth. She would need to forgive herself before she could really open her arms to her child.

It's amazing how often Jesus speaks of forgiveness. It seems that we have to get this one right. John Pilch says in his book *The Cultural Dictionary of the Bible* (Liturgical Press, 1999) that in the first century the honor/shame system bound people to vengeance. If you didn't avenge a wrong done to you then you were shamed. "The person who forgives," Pilch says, "forgoes vengeance and freely offers to restore the mutual relationship to its appropriate state."

Jesus suggests here again that we break the cultural boundaries and forgive without limit. He knew that if we did not forgive then we would be inhibited from being in communion with the community and with God. Peter's great sin of denial led to great forgiveness. Once Peter felt the forgiveness of Jesus and his own, he was free to show great love and strength. He

was free to become the "rock" on whom Jesus would build his
church (Matthew16:18).

> *When they had finished breakfast,*
> *Jesus said to Simon Peter,*
> *"Simon son of John, do you love me more than these?"*
> *He said to him, "Yes, Lord;*
> *you know that I love you. . . ."*
> *He said to him the third time,*
> *"Simon son of John, do you love me?"*
> JOHN 21:15–17

13

Judgments

Let us therefore no longer pass judgment on one another,
but resolve instead never to put a stumbling block
or hindrance in the way of another.
ROMANS 14:13

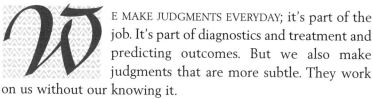 E MAKE JUDGMENTS EVERYDAY; it's part of the job. It's part of diagnostics and treatment and predicting outcomes. But we also make judgments that are more subtle. They work on us without our knowing it.

I've been disturbed lately because we have had a mother bringing in her breast milk for her infant but it smells of alcohol. She's an educated, upper-middle-class white woman from the very "right" part of town. No one has confronted her with the question and the potential problem of drinking while breast-feeding. She also has other children at home. Is she drinking while caring for them? Should we continue to give her breast milk to her infant if we think it contains alcohol? Are we all just assuming that nothing is wrong at home because she looks so together, so like one of us?

If she had a different profile, I wonder if many of us in the unit would make different assumptions and intervene more aggressively. If we are hesitant to confront this mother with these types of issues, are we ignoring a cry for help? Are we denying her and her child the services that are available and appropriate for them? Will we put the children at risk because we don't want to question our own assumptions that an educated woman of means is able to handle her own problems or doesn't have any problems? Do our prejudices and judgments lead to errors in our care for these patients and their families?

JUDGMENTS ARE MADE so often without asking questions; they are just assumed. One of the most constant ideas in the meal stories is Jesus' warning against judgments, those same assumptions we all make. There are ten meal stories in the gospel of Luke; each deals with a preconceived judgment in one way or another. During the meal at the house of Levi, the Pharisees can't imagine why Jesus would eat with sinners and tax collectors. In that culture you remained pure by disassociating yourself from anyone who was judged to be impure. Separation was the unquestioned rule. Jesus, however, does not judge Levi or his tax collector friends. Instead he eats with them, which meant he was in solidarity with them.

It is a similar story at the next meal in the house of Simon. The woman "who was a sinner" washes Jesus' feet with her tears; instead of shunning her, Jesus praises her. The Pharisees even question Jesus' ability as a prophet because they think he is missing the obvious judgment—that she is a bad woman. During the meal at the house of Mary and Martha, it's Mary who doesn't fit the mold. In that culture and until very recently in our own, it was assumed that women should be in the kitchen. Jesus did not hold to this assumption and affirmed Mary in her decision to stay with him.

During the next meal at the house of a Pharisee, Jesus doesn't follow the purification rules of washing before eating. Here he tells the Pharisee that the rules are secondary to the people of God. And although Jesus repeatedly warned against riches, he does not prejudge the rich man who had been just in his dealings with others. Instead, Jesus congratulates him and tells him that he is close to the kingdom of heaven.

It goes on and on like this in all of the gospels. Though Jesus was a good Jewish boy, he did not judge people by the standards with which he was raised. In each meal story, instead of making judgments, Jesus remained open to the possibility of doing things in a different way, coming to a new conclusion. He questioned the assumptions, even his own.

I HAVE CONDUCTED training sessions for eucharistic ministers many times in the past twenty years, and each time the question arises about serving someone communion if you know they are not Catholic. The church feels that Eucharist should be restricted to Catholics because we supposedly believe in the same fundamental things about the Eucharist. We are in solidarity with each other. Of course, we don't know each person's private beliefs. We don't know if someone is in a state of mortal sin either and that too is a restriction.

Looking at all of the meal stories and especially the Last Supper accounts, I don't see how Eucharist could ever be interpreted as anything but a meal open to all. In fact, it seems that in restricting the meal we do the opposite of what Jesus repeated throughout the meals. The most obvious example is during the Last Supper. This meal and the one in John 21:9-14 are the only meals where Jesus is the host. At the other meals Jesus is a guest. Even the "feeding of the multitude" stories depict Jesus as a guide to the disciples who are really the acting hosts.

The Last Supper seems to be the culmination and combination of all the other meals. Jesus sees to the preparations and leads the meal. This time he is inviting us to his table and it seems to be the example he wants us to follow. He breaks the bread and says it is given for all and that the wine, his blood, is poured out for many. His table was not restricted to people of status or education. He did not restrict on the grounds of hair color or skin color, not even on whether the person was in good standing with the church. At a time when the whole temple system was based on judgments of who was righteous and who was a sinner, Jesus welcomed us all to his table. He reiterated in action the words he spoke at the house of Levi: "I did not come to call the righteous, but the sinners." And that is all of us.

Many of the great spiritual leaders recommend praying the psalms or praying with poetry. I have always had difficulty with this, and I realize it's because I try to read using only my language center in the left side of the brain. I know what's coming in the next line or I can fill in the blanks. But with poetry we have to use a different part of the brain, the right side, not just the language center. The right side is more attuned to imagery and rhythm. Poetry is less predictable and assumptions are more difficult.

I mentioned before that I had missed the true meaning of the story about forgiveness and love because of my presuppositions. During that meal Jesus tells us that forgiveness produces great love instead of what I assumed, that great love allows forgiveness. There is a similar twist here. I was taught that we come to the table if and when our belief system is correct and if we are in a state of grace. But I think the opposite is really the case. It is in coming to the table that we feel forgiven and received. Then we can start to understand and believe the gifts of the incarnation, the resurrection, and the necessity of the cross.

It is not because we have been transformed therefore that we are permitted at the table. Jesus welcomes us to the table so that we may be healed and transformed. Jesus has broken the rules, dismissed the assumptions, so that we are all welcome at his table.

Love your enemies
and pray for those who persecute you,
so that you may be children
of your Father in heaven;
for he makes his sun rise on the evil
and on the good,
and sends rain on the righteous
and on the unrighteous. . . .
Be perfect, therefore,
as your heavenly Father is perfect.
MATTHEW 5:44–45, 48

14

Living Water, Bread of Life

Jesus said to them, "I am the bread of life.
Whoever comes to me will never be hungry,
and whoever believes in me will never be thirsty."
JOHN 6:35

N INTERESTING PARADOX is that the table is where intimacy is established and where the loss of intimacy is most evident. At the Last Supper, how difficult it must have been for Jesus to dip his bread in the same bowl with Judas knowing that "Satan [had] entered into him" and he would betray him. They had been together for so long they knew each other; they had become family. How many meals they must have shared on the road together.

I wonder how Jesus felt being handed over by one of his own. I can imagine the deep sorrow and disappointment in his face, the cracking in his voice as he told Judas to "do quickly what you are going to do" (John 13:27). I wonder if Jesus could not stand to be with Judas any longer in that close environment of deeply committed friends.

The table and food are emotionally charged. We associate the food we eat with relationships. "Comfort food" is comfortable because it brings back memories of a certain person or time. A friend of mine told me that her comfort food is macaroni and a hot dog. Whenever she or her children feel under the weather they break out the macs and dogs. I asked her who made that for her and when. Betty told me about her grandmother and how she would always make that meal for her. The macaroni had to be made in a particular way and then it did the trick. Now her children associate the same foods with the comfort and love they receive from their mother.

It's no wonder that families and even cultures end up having foods that are specific to them. Even the advertisers picked up on it. Years ago there was a commercial with a boy and his father walking down a long lonely hallway after the child's team had just lost the hockey game. The dad didn't need to say anything; he just put his arm around the child and offered him a lifesaver.

My comfort food is cinnamon toast. An older woman was my mother's helper when we were all still young children. She was like a grandmother to us. Each morning when Mary was there, I would get up early so I could slip downstairs and have tea and toast with her. She would be sitting at the kitchen table; barely looking up she would say, "Hi, Doll," as I walked into the room. There was always a cup and plate waiting just in case I woke up and came to join her. In our house the quiet times with just one or two were rare and this was one of those times. I felt special.

ALTHOUGH FOOD IS ASSOCIATED with relationships, it is not a substitute. We know from many studies that infants can be fed but will not thrive without physical contact from a caring person. Even voices from a television will not soothe them. At first they will cry for attention. After days or weeks of effort they stop crying and start to wither, even if their nutritional needs are being met. Most of the bonding between a parent and infant occurs during feeding. The infant seems to know that this time is the foundation for life. Association with food can also be the thing that painfully exhibits the lack of relationship or intimacy in life.

I have noticed how many people with "eating disorders" say that they are trying to fill an empty place inside of them with food. If they eat enough then somehow they will be filled. But of course it's not the food that's lacking, it's love and all that flows from it. It's a space that can never be filled by anything except a loving relationship. Some people stop eating when under severe stress. When I was in college I was admitted into the infirmary with dehydration during exam week my junior year. I was convinced that I needed to get perfect scores on my exams so I stayed up for many days and nights studying. I was so nervous that I couldn't eat.

We all react differently to stressful situations but the ones involving relationships seem to bring our emotions closest to the surface. If my husband and I are fighting I will sit at the table, but the food tastes like rocks in my mouth. I can't swallow it.

Some people who have been referred to me for a swallowing study describe difficulty not with textures of food but with the circumstances surrounding the food. They have difficulty in certain places or with certain people or when eating alone. It may be that the difficulty started with a specific traumatic event. Often the symptoms are variable and we ask them to keep a log of when and what they eat so we can help them see the patterns. When the tests show no physical deficits

I am not surprised. It's the event, the situation that the meal has been associated with, that is causing the swallowing difficulty. The meal has pointed out a far deeper problem.

The story of the woman at the well (John 4:4) speaks to us about eating and drinking but never about being filled. It's the emptiness inside that can never be satisfied. When Jesus offers the woman living water, he is offering a relationship with God. He says, "I'll be your comfort food." It is the relationship that is fulfilling and will well up inside her so that she will never thirst again. A few minutes later he tells his disciples when they plead with him to eat something, "I have food to eat that you do not know about (John 4:32)." He says that doing the will of the Father is his food. Being in the Father and the Father in him gives him life-sustaining nourishment. It is the availability of this relationship that he is trying to give to us all.

> *". . . but those who drink of the water*
> *that I will give them will never be thirsty.*
> *The water that I will give will become in them*
> *a spring of water gushing up to eternal life."*
> JOHN 4:14

15

True Presence

[Jesus] said to them, "Are you discussing among yourselves
what I meant when I said,
'A little while, and you will no longer see me,
and again a little while, and you will see me'?
Very truly, I tell you, you will weep and mourn,
but the world will rejoice; you will have pain,
but your pain will turn into joy."
JOHN 16:19-20

"Go therefore and make disciples of all nations,
baptizing them . . . and teaching them
to obey everything that I have commanded you.
And remember, I am with you always,
to the end of the age."
MATTHEW 28:19-20

HAVE HEARD AND READ SO OFTEN how important it is
to live in the present. We can only meet God in the
present. But my personality has such difficulty with
living only in this moment. I do not live in the past
but I am always planning for the future. I have one foot here
and one foot there.

Today I saw an amazing example of living in the present. One of our young moms was diagnosed with a very aggressive cancer during her pregnancy. She carried the baby as long as she could but he was delivered about seven weeks early. He is doing well; unfortunately, mom is not. Although they are treating the cancer now, her prognosis is guarded. She knows that her time with her newborn son is likely to be limited. She may not see his first birthday.

What is truly amazing about her is that she did not seem sad or anxious. She was grateful for each piece of good news about her son and was content to sit and hold him as he slept. Today she was saying that she was scheduled for some procedures and so wouldn't be able to get out of bed for a couple of days. She said that she would be back into the nursery as soon as she could move around. Then she looked down at her son saying, "but I'm here now."

I wondered if she was still talking to me or just to her son and if she meant that simple phrase in a more profound way. This mom was not only visiting her child, she was determined to be truly present to him for as long as she could. This moment was the only moment.

When we are truly present it is not only a state of being physically in the area but also a state of mind, heart, and soul. How many times have I been present in body only? How many moments have I sleep-walked through? How many times have I missed the readings at church because my mind is still back at the house trying to get the kids dressed and in the car? I have wished away so much time waiting for the weekend or for the holiday coming up. I can't get to sleep at night sometimes because I am trying to solve the world's problems or I am mulling over something I could have done differently that day.

By my example, I'm sure my children do the same. They can't wait until lunch or homework, or something else is over so they can go out to play. How much of my life has been wished away? If only I could take on the attitude of this mother and others who are facing death. Would I live every moment? Would I be able to say, "I'm here now" and mean it? Jesus promised, "I am with you always, to the end of the age" (Matthew 28:20).

I would have been like so many of the disciples, asking him how we would know his presence. I think they wanted clues so they would recognize him in the future, when he returned. Instead he told them to look for him now in the present moment. He said we could recognize him in the least of the brothers and sisters. He said where two of us were gathered he would be there. And that he would be present when we shared his meal. He promised that he would always be here now.

A friend asked me to help her with an article she was writing for our church newsletter about the doctrine of the "true presence." She was discussing the results of a survey taken a number of years ago, which revealed that most Catholics don't believe in the "true presence" of Christ in the Eucharist. The doctrine has been debated since the first century. The question is: "Is Christ really present in the bread and wine?" Among other things, the Catholic Church points to Jesus' words during the Last Supper when he gives the disciples the bread and wine and tells them "This is my body; take it and eat it; and this is my blood. . ." (Mark 14:22, 24).

These words are repeated in one form or another in all the synoptic gospels. Believing that the God who created the universe chooses to be present in bread and wine is not a big leap of faith for me. He is God after all. I think if it were examined carefully we would find that the difficulty comes in believing that he is present in us and to us. If we believe that Jesus is present in the Eucharist, which we consume, how can we then deny his presence in us? Jesus said "Those who eat my flesh and drink my blood abide in me, and I in them" (John 6:56).

This is the tough part. Maybe we need to repeat it every week in order to start believing it. The leap of faith is in believing that we are also divine beings. If we believed in the divine nature in all of us, would we be more present to each other, not only in church but also later in the parking lot? Is that why Jesus said we would know him when we encountered the least of our brothers, in gatherings of believers, and at his meal? God is not to be found in the past or in the future. He is encountered in each other, in all things, in the present moment; and so we must live there also.

For me it is not a question of God's presence. Of course he is present. The question I must ask myself is "Am I present, mind, body, and spirit, to the presence of God?" If I am then I will be transformed.

After my aunt lost her husband a few years ago she sent this poem to me. She said it was something she needed to be reminded of and that it brought her great comfort. I read it now almost every day to remind myself to live in the present moment.

I Am

I was regretting the past
And fearing the future.
Suddenly my Lord was speaking:
"My name is I Am." He paused,
I waited. He continued,
"When you live in the past,
With its mistakes and regrets,
It is hard. I am not there.
My name is not I Was.
When you live in the future,
With its problems and fears,
It is hard. I am not there.
My name is not I Will Be.
When you live in this moment,

It is not hard. I am here.
My name is I AM.
AUTHOR UNKNOWN

Breathing in, I calm my body.
Breathing out, I smile.
Dwelling in the present moment,
I know this is a wonderful moment.
BUDDHIST PRAYER

16

God's Voice

*And when you turn to the right
or when you turn to the left,
your ears shall hear a word behind you,
saying, "This is the way; walk in it."*
ISAIAH 30:21

BEFORE THE PARENTS OF OUR INFANT PATIENTS can appreciate the complexity of feeding they need to understand the world in which their baby lives. I explain that infants who are born prematurely have an underdeveloped sensory system. They can take in information—hear, see, smell and feel—but they cannot filter the information. It all comes to them as if it is equally important. They can't filter out the monitor alarms in order to attend to their parent's voice. If the environment is full of lights and noise and movement, they can't cope. It's too much for them and they become disorganized.

One way they show the stress is by holding their arms out and splaying their fingers—it looks like the policeman's sign for "stop." This is exactly what they're trying to say. If we ignore this stress sign they will continue to call for help with a series of movement patterns or finally their heart rate and oxygen level will drop. If the environment is too stimulating then the child does not have the resources to attend to the feeding.

As I gave this little talk again today, I felt like adding, "You know we don't change very much as we get older, we just don't pay attention to our own stress signs." I tell the parents that if we give them an environment in which to learn, in time their infant will gain the skills they need to filter. We need an environment where we, too, can learn. We are bombarded with multiple stimuli simultaneously and instead of showing our stress and decreasing the stimuli, so often we ignore our own red flags and just become accustomed to the noise.

I have a hard time determining which stimulus I should attend to. Which of the many voices should I listen to? How can I hear the voice of God within all the activity and noise of my life? The Evil One doesn't have to coax us into sin, all he has to do is throw in some noise to dull our senses. God talks to us all the time; we just can't filter out all that noise so we don't recognize it. Eventually we can become numb and, like the infants, we can't always determine what is important and what is just noise.

I remember going on a silent retreat once. It was five days of quiet—no phone, no television, no books (except the Bible), no work, and no interruptions. Once a day the schedule permitted a few minutes when we talked with our spiritual director, but otherwise no communication with anyone. We didn't even have a clock. I woke up and went to bed when the mood hit me. There were no schedules to keep and really no expectations. The first couple of days were difficult. I had so much to do back home and was anxious because I couldn't get to it.

Once I finally settled in, I started to notice a change. Instead of deciding how I would get something done, I was able to think about whether it should be done. I had the time to ponder. I stopped making lists in my mind. I stopped trying to analyze people. I spent hours just sitting. I don't even remember thinking about much. I started to notice little things around me. I listened to the birds and the wind and the stream. I lay on the ground like a kid and watched the clouds move. I had long quiet conversations with God.

It's as close as I've come to feeling like "the beloved disciple" of John's gospel, who during the Last Supper lay back on Jesus' chest to feel his heartbeat and hear him whisper. It didn't seem like a life-changing experience until I got back to the "real world." When I returned to home and work, the auditory, visual, mental, and emotional noise was deafening. I was so overwhelmed with the activity that it was hard to think. Ever since then, I have longed to go back—not to the place, but to that space where I learned to stop and listen and feel.

AT THE WEDDING AT CANA the headwaiter noticed that the family saved the choice wine for last. Usually the good wine was served first. After the guests start to get a little drunk, when their senses are dulled, then the poorer wine would be served. By the end of the party they couldn't differentiate the good wine from the bad. The dancing, the music, and the many conversations going on at the same time also dulled their senses. It only says that the headwaiter recognized the vintage wine and he of course was confused by its sudden appearance.

The servants and a few disciples knew a little more, they had witnessed the miracle. They were separated from the activity so they could see what had really happened. The grace of the miracle was there in the transformation of the water made into vintage wine, wine that was tasted by all. With their senses dulled they failed to recognize the miracle. Yet it was still a miracle, still grace; but it seems from the story that most of the people at the party never recognized it. They were distracted by all the activity.

At the other end of Jesus' ministry when he is on the cross, he is offered sour wine. Some scholars say that the Last Supper hadn't really ended until this point drawing together the Last Supper and the crucifixion as one event. They site the traditional Passover liturgy with its four cups of wine. Jesus and his disciples go through it until the third cup, which is followed by a Psalm, but instead of finishing the ritual, they walk out into the night. In John's gospel, while on the cross, Jesus takes a sip of the sour wine and says, "It is finished"—the final cup and words of the ritual. Yet in the other gospels it says that Jesus refuses a wine and myrrh mixture.

I believe these accounts point out something different. At the time, the bitter mixture was used as a sort of anesthetic to dull the pain. I believe Jesus refused to have his senses dulled. He chose to be awake, to feel life and death. In those final moments I believe he heard God's comforting voice. In the introductory story of his ministry, their dulled senses keep the partygoers from the full goodness of life. In the final story, Jesus could allow the dulling of his senses to avoid pain. Instead, he chooses to take the bitter and the sweet.

In the silence, without all the distractions to dull my senses, I think I may feel the pain more, maybe the pain of the world. There too I will feel joy in hearing the voice of God.

Before you speak it is necessary for you to listen,
for God speaks in the silence of the heart.
MOTHER TERESA

17

Transformation

Do not be conformed to this world,
but be transformed by the renewing of your minds,
so that you may discern what is the will of God—
what is good and acceptable and perfect.
ROMANS 12:2

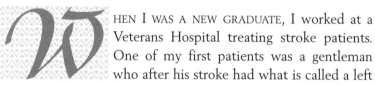HEN I WAS A NEW GRADUATE, I worked at a Veterans Hospital treating stroke patients. One of my first patients was a gentleman who after his stroke had what is called a left neglect. This sided neglect is common after a stroke and it causes the patient to be totally unaware of their weak side. For them the body stops at the midline. When testing Mr. Ellis, he correctly pointed to the objects toward the right side of the table but did not answer at all when I asked him to point to the ones on the left. The neglect was so complete that he didn't even try to turn his head to explore the possibility of a larger environment.

From him I learned a few things about this kind of disability. First, that it is total. You can't convince them that the left side of the body or the environment exists. Second, if you point out the neglected side you also point out all of their deficits. It is very difficult to discover that you not only have this other side, but also to realize that your arm and your leg don't move, that your face droops and you're drooling. If the person comes to this realization too quickly there is the danger of their falling into hopelessness and depression. It is their darkest night.

During eating they are at risk to aspirate because they can't control the food or liquid going down the weak side of the mouth and throat and their body doesn't react to the aspirated material. Physiologically it is vital for recovery that the patient becomes aware of this and works toward integration of the neglected side, but it has to be in small steps. We can't start to rehabilitate those parts of the body until the patient starts to attend to them. Only after some time, we bring in a mirror to get full awareness and use it to help them learn to integrate their weak side. Finally, they begin to see all the capabilities that they do have, often ones they were unaware of before.

THE SAME IS TRUE in the spiritual and psychological realm. We all "neglect" our weak side, and for much of our lives are probably totally unaware of it. I know that has been true for me. The parallels between the neglect of my "dark side"—Jung calls it the shadow—with the behavior of my patients have been startling. I am skilled at ignoring characteristics I don't like in myself but at the same time being able to see them quite clearly in others. Jesus knows his psychology 101 when he tells us to take the log out of our own eye before we try to take the sliver out of the eye of our neighbor.

I learned a tool called the Enneagram, which is used to identify personality characteristics and for personal and spiritual growth. When I finally admitted that I was in fact a particular type, I felt like crying. I had to confront and acknowledge that there are parts of my personality I don't like and probably never will.

Like the stroke victim who realizes his deficits all at once, I recognized so many of my failings and faults that I felt there must be no hope for me. The saving grace was that I believe in saving grace. Being a therapist I knew that attention to my weaknesses was the first step to bringing balance and integration to my life. I've heard that the Buddhist temple is made up of many rooms with an inner room, which is starkly empty. In the center there is a mirror. I think they have it right. We need to go through many rooms of self-discovery before we can go deep enough and look at ourselves in the mirror and see who we really are.

It is when I can no longer juggle all the roles I play that I remember my need for caring and forgiveness. Like my patients, I have had to grieve the loss of the strong successful person I thought I was and come to accept myself as flawed and weak. So many spiritual writers have said that transformation comes during the dark night of the soul. It comes in the shape of the cross. We must pass through death before resurrection. I have seen this to be true at times in my own life.

One of the most difficult times, when I had to face the very real possibility that my marriage might not survive, I was forced to mature and grow in faith. I had to determine what was really important to me and let go of the idea that I could make life "happily ever after." I am grateful that there have also been a few transforming moments which have come out of joy and even laughter.

There are times when I have laughed at myself, when I have realized just how little I am. I was the smallest of ten kids but I would fight my very formidable father more than any of them. He told me that as a toddler I would look way up at him (standing with my hands on my hips) and say, "You can't make me." It didn't seem to matter what he was asking me to do. I just wanted the ground rules to be understood. I was the master of my fate.

DURING MY EARLY DAYS at work I would become depressed when I saw patients who I knew that I could not help. They were too sick, too weak, or not cognizant enough for therapy to be effective. I would search for some way to help, to fix, to cure. I found after many sleepless nights pouring over books and journals, that what I needed to do was allow God to care for them. I could not control, fix, or cure.

Out of the frustration and impotence I realized that it was not about me. I had to be there for my patient without being able to do anything, just be. I had to laugh at myself that it took sheer exhaustion to make me give up something that I had no control over in the first place. That's when I could start to pray for and with my patients and realize that they were in far better hands than my own. I think those are the times when I become more of a healer.

In her book *When The Heart Waits* (HarperCollins, 1992), Sue Monk Kidd talks about choosing a symbol for yourself. In prayer one day I could visualize that my symbol would be a sailboat and in that moment I congratulated myself because I was determined to allow God to be the captain of my ship. It was an epiphany. I was really giving of myself now. But the next day my silent meditation was interrupted with my own laughter. I had to laugh out loud at myself. I had been visualizing my sailboat and welcoming God to be my captain but suddenly I knew he was saying, "I don't want to be the captain of your ship; that's too small. My spirit is the wind, put up your sail and come with me."

When the disciples were at their lowest point, after the death of Jesus, they were confused, hopeless and grieving. Their dreams had been shattered; their Lord was dead. But out of that fear and darkness in that upper room, Jesus came and ate with them. Jesus was anxious to eat with them. It seems that in eating, Jesus could reassure them that he was not a dream, that he was the reality.

It's the reoccurring mystery of faith—before the resurrection there is the cross; out of the darkness came a great light. God has been most evident to me in the darkness. The insight, the bright light of knowing, or the feeling of being comforted or forgiven have come in times of darkness. Maybe we need those times of darkness so we can see the light of God in our lives. I think the light is always there but like the stars that fade with the sunrise, grace is difficult to see when my ego is in the way.

While in the darkness I have an attitude of searching, trying to find my way. I become vigilant and observant. The flash of light is bright because I am attuned to it. If only I could carry that attitude with me always, searching, being responsive to any indication that God is near. I'm sure I would be overwhelmed with the magnitude of his presence. I must accept the responsibility of using my strengths for building the kingdom, while recognizing that my weaknesses are what bring me to God. I must learn to appreciate the night and know that the stars will come out to guide me. Through the laughter and the tears, I learn to be my best self because it is then that God is the wind in my sail and I follow.

> Oh God, grant that I may understand that it is you
> who are painfully parting the fibers of my being
> in order to penetrate to the very marrow of my substance
> and bear me away within yourself.
> TEILHARD DE CHARDIN, *THE DIVINE MILIEU*

Afterword

*The activity of God is everywhere and always present,
but it is visible only to the eye of faith.*

JEAN-PIERRE DE CAUSSADE

A s I STARTED TO EXAMINE MY LIFE in prayer I found that God was popping up everywhere. He was not limited to a church. He could not be compartmentalized. We may try to separate church and state but we cannot separate out God. He will get to us wherever we are.

In an essay about the authority of the Bible, Thomas Merton writes: "The 'Word of God' is recognized in actual experience because it does something to anyone who really hears it." I have become convinced that God reveals himself to us each day in seemingly ordinary events. And further, each of our lives tells a story of God. The Bible is full of such stories. When we share our stories with each other we can begin to see that the men and women of the Bible are still with us. Those stories are not just myths of the past that have no relationship to us today. Those men and women were like us. They were living ordinary lives, trying to teach their kids right from wrong, support their families, and get along with the neighbors. Like us, they too were searching for the universal truths, the meaning of life, and unconditional love.

The good news is that we don't have to go searching for the answers to the big questions or our yearnings—they are already with us. They can be found in the story of our lives. Jesus used the everyday activities of work, parenting, paying the bills, and, of course, eating together not only as a memorable and under-standable way to teach but in a broader sense to say that God is infused in all the aspects of our lives. He is the answer to all of our questions and yearnings.

LOOKING AT MY OWN LIFE in relationship to scripture has given me a new appreciation for the Bible. The scripture stories have become my stories and my story has been joined to theirs. I have become more aware of God's presence. I have come to believe that God would have us lift the veil between the sacred and the secular and see grace everywhere. In this effort we will come to honor our lives as creations of God, as he honors the life he made in us.

My vocation is not to be daughter, sister, wife, mother, speech pathologist, or lay minister. My vocation is to live the incarnation as Christ taught us. It is my vocation to carry an image of God to others through all of my roles. My roles are only a means to an end. They are the means by which God communicates; the end is to reveal God in all things. I believe that to live the incarnation is the vocation of all Christians.

My Lord God, I have no idea where I am going.
I do not see the road ahead of me.
I cannot know for certain where it will end.
Nor do I really know myself,
and the fact that I think I am following your will
does not mean that I am actually doing so.
But I believe that the desire to please you
does in fact please you.
And I hope I have that desire in all that I am doing.

I hope that I will never do anything apart from that desire.
And I know that if I do this
you will lead me by the right road,
though I may know nothing about it.
Therefore I will trust you always
though I may seem to be lost and in the shadow of death.
I will not fear, for you are ever with me,
and you will never leave me to face my perils alone.

THOMAS MERTON

Kathleen Casey received her B.S. in Speech Pathology and Audiology from James Madison University in Virginia in 1982 and her Masters in Speech Pathology from the University of Virginia in 1984. She is the clinical coordinator of speech pathology at a Richmond hospital where she has served for twelve years. Ms. Casey is also an adjunct professor at JMU where she teaches a class in pediatric dysphagia. She is married to Thom and they have two children, Michele and Brian.